ONCE Upon a RHYME

SOMERSET & DORSET

Edited by Donna Samworth

First published in Great Britain in 2011 by:

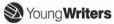 Young**Writers**

Young Writers
Remus House
Coltsfoot Drive
Peterborough
PE2 9BF
Telephone: 01733 890066
Website: www.youngwriters.co.uk

THIS BOOK BELONGS TO

....

Foreword

Here at Young Writers our objective is to help children discover the joys of poetry and creative writing. Few things are more encouraging for the aspiring writer than seeing their own work in print. We are proud that our anthologies are able to give young authors this unique sense of confidence and pride in their abilities.

Once Upon A Rhyme is our latest fantastic competition, specifically designed to encourage the writing skills of primary school children through the medium of poetry. From the high quality of entries received, it is clear that Once Upon A Rhyme really captured the imagination of all involved.

The resulting collection is an excellent showcase for the poetic talents of the younger generation and we are sure you will be charmed and inspired by it, both now and in the future.

Stoberry Park School, Wells

The Epiphany School, Bournemouth

Wellington Junior School, Wellington

Windwhistle Primary School, Weston-super-Mare

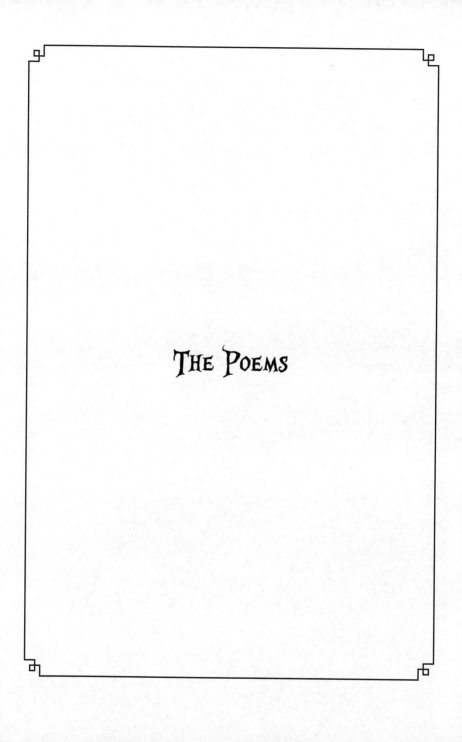

THE POEMS

Friends

Friends are fun
Friends are cool
Friends are helpful
Some are cruel
But when you're sad
And need some fun
They are there like a ray of sun.

Lewis Taylor (8)

If I Was A Rocket

If I was a rocket
I would race comets
To the end of time.

If I was a rocket
I would hurtle through soulless galaxies
Like a raging hurricane.

If I was a rocket
I would whizz through a lost galaxy
Like a child looking for their mother.

If I was a rocket
I would dine with the suns
And dance with dwarf planets.

If I was a rocket
I would ice skate
On Saturn's icy rings.

Maddie Evans (9)
Ashcombe Primary School, Weston-super-Mare

What Is The Earth?

The Earth is a massive blob of mint bubblegum and vanilla ice cream
Lost in a never-ending ebony shadow.

It is a swirly emerald and sapphire lollipop
Lost in the darkness of the space.

It is an enormous blue and green shiny bowling ball
In a jet-black velvet cushion.

It is a massive shimmering jade and indigo football
On an endless jet-black football pitch.

It is a gigantic azure and emerald gem
In a relentless black hole.

Reece Ferguson (9)
Ashcombe Primary School, Weston-super-Mare

If I Was A Rocket

If I was a rocket
I would zoom around planets
As fast as lightning.

If I was a rocket
I would zoom around like a firework.

If I was a rocket
I would race comets like a lion
Catching its prey.

If I was a rocket
I would zoom in and out of different galaxies.

If I was a rocket
I would blast off launch pads
Like a speeding jet.

Christopher John Barnett (10)
Ashcombe Primary School, Weston-super-Mare

If I Was A Rocket

If I was a rocket
I would orbit the planets
Like the Earth does to the sun.

If I was a rocket
I would zoom around space
As fast as a shooting star.

If I was a rocket
I would whizz through space
Searching for new planets.

If I was a rocket
I would find out if there is life
On any planets.

If I was a rocket
I would zoom through space
Passing by the planets as if I was in a maze.

Eva Ferdinando (9)
Ashcombe Primary School, Weston-super-Mare

What Is The Earth?

Earth is like a blue and green football that floats
Into the darkness of space.

Earth is like a giant volleyball hit into space,
Swishing and twirling.

Earth is like wicked blue diamond high
In the air, orbiting the sun.

Earth is like a round clock floating in space.

Earth is like a big giant's marble
Swishing in the air.

Jaylan Bacon (10)
Ashcombe Primary School, Weston-super-Mare

If I Was A Rocket

If I was a rocket
I would blast through space as
Fast as lightning.

If I was a rocket
I would shoot past asteroids
Chasing the stars.

If I was a rocket
I would zoom through comets
Like a racing car.

If I was a rocket
I would chase aliens away to
The end of galaxies.

If I was a rocket
I would zigzag through different planets.

Ria Osborne (9)
Ashcombe Primary School, Weston-super-Mare

If I Was A Rocket

If I was a rocket
I would zoom round the darkness of space
Orbiting the sun.

If I was a rocket
I would race with comets to the end of
The solar system.

If I was a rocket
I would skate on the rings of Saturn.

If I was a rocket
I would race to the moon and back.

If I was a rocket
I would zoom to Milky Way and back.

Leah Spence Harrhy (9)
Ashcombe Primary School, Weston-super-Mare

If I Was A Rocket

If I was a rocket
I would whizz round looking for signs of life
Like a lion hunting for his prey.

If I was a rocket
I would zoom around looking
For new universes.

If I was a rocket
I would skate on Saturn's icy rings
Like an ice skater.

If I was a rocket
I would race comets
And asteroids.

If I was a rocket
I would chase aliens
Like a shooting star.

Olivia Farler (9)
Ashcombe Primary School, Weston-super-Mare

If I Was A Star

If I was a star
I would shoot around the night sky
Like a bullet.

If I was a star
I would make friends in the Milky Way
And sing lullabies to the Earthling babies.

If I was a star
I would dance around the universe
Like a dainty silver lady.

If I was a star
I would twinkle really bright
Like the fiery sun.

If I was a star
I would race comets
To the edge of the universe.

Lucy Loud (9)
Ashcombe Primary School, Weston-super-Mare

If I Was A Rocket

If I was a rocket
I would shoot up to the stars
I would do loop the loops and discover life on Mars.

If I was a rocket
I would zoom higher and higher in the sky
I would go faster than a comet, well at least I would try.

If I was a rocket
I would go to a Martian show
Then I would visit my favourite planet, and then I would visit Pluto.

If I was a rocket
I would gaze at a star coming to the end of its life
It would be quite scary and I would have to dodge the points
As sharp as a knife.

If I was a rocket
I would be running out of power
I will have to land soon but first one last visit to the moon.

Alice Morgan (9)
Ashcombe Primary School, Weston-super-Mare

What Is The Earth?

The Earth is an abstract art with only azure and jade
Lost in a puddle of ink.

It is bubblegum and mint ice cream
Hiding in the depths of a dark room.

It is an azure eye
Gazing out of a pitch-black cave.

It is an indigo and emerald plate
Standing out on a dark tray.

It is a blue and green marble
Nestling on the darkest velvet cushion.

Matthew Haydn (10)
Ashcombe Primary School, Weston-super-Mare

If I Was A Rocket

If I was a rocket
I would speed like a bullet
To a different galaxy.

If I was a rocket
I would zoom to Pluto
Like a fighter jet in the war.

If I was a rocket
I would orbit the sun
Like a sleepy tornado.

If I was a rocket
I would play a game of dodgeball
With the asteroids.

If I was a rocket
I would visit the moon
And take him a cake for tea.

Daniel Hassell (9)
Ashcombe Primary School, Weston-super-Mare

What Is Earth?

The Earth is an emerald balloon
Lost in the wilderness of a chalk board.

The Earth is a sphere-coloured emerald
Sapphire in a pitch-black cave.

It is as round as a green pumpkin
Lost in the darkness of night.

It is a big ice cream scoop
Glooming on a black pillow on your bed.

It is a giant football kicked up in space
Coloured a shiny jade and green.

Carrick Flint (10)
Ashcombe Primary School, Weston-super-Mare

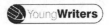

What Is The Earth?

The Earth is a blue and green circle
That floats in the darkness of space.

It is a sapphire and emerald lollipop
Hiding under a velvet cushion.

It is a glitter ball
That sits in the dark air.

It is a shimmering jade and emerald earring
That sits in mid-air.

It is a green tennis ball
Being hit into a lost cave.

It is a turquoise snow globe

It is an indigo and azure gem
On a pair of dark curtains.

Tayla Pollard (9)
Ashcombe Primary School, Weston-super-Mare

What Is The Earth?

The Earth is an emerald marble
Lost in an unlit cave.

It is a blue and green disco ball
Floating on a black velvet cushion.

It is an emerald thumb print
Lost in a starless sky.

It is a blue and green football
Hidden in a pair of black curtains.

It is an emerald and blue gem
Staring out from a pitch-black cave.

Matthew Walsh (10)
Ashcombe Primary School, Weston-super-Mare

If I Was A Rocket

If I was a rocket
I would glide through space
Orbiting the planets.

If I was a rocket
I would follow the planets
To see where they get to.

If I was a rocket
I would hurtle through
The starless shadow of the galaxies.

If I was a rocket
I would run away from the asteroids
Like the comets zooming to a new planet.

If I was a rocket
I would touch every galaxy.

Mia McIntyre (9)
Ashcombe Primary School, Weston-super-Mare

If I Was A Rocket

If I was a rocket
I would glide like a puppet being
Swayed in space.

If I was a rocket
I would zoom around planets like a
Tiger looking for meat.

If I was a rocket
I would race comets like a horse in a race.

If I was a rocket
I would zoom around the moon like a dog chasing a cat.

If I was a rocket
I would chase shooting stars like a lion chasing its prey.

Katie Chester (10)
Ashcombe Primary School, Weston-super-Mare

If I Was A Rocket

If I was a rocket
I would zoom around the planets
Like an exploding firework.

If I was a rocket
I would look for Martians through
My enormous telescope.

If I was a rocket
I would zigzag through planets
Like a racing car.

If I was a rocket
I would whizz around the galaxies
Like a shooting star.

If I was a rocket
I would zoom around the stars.

Ruby Spurling (10)
Ashcombe Primary School, Weston-super-Mare

If I Was A Rocket

If I was a rocket
I would shoot up through the atmosphere,
As fast as a cannonball.

If I was a rocket
I would hurtle through space racing comets
And asteroids, to the edge of the universe.

If I was a rocket
I would feast with the twinkling moons and
Dance with the shining stars.

If I was a rocket
I would journey through the universe, discovering new planets
And discovering people who live there.

George Skeen (9)
Ashcombe Primary School, Weston-super-Mare

The Earth

The Earth is a silent comet
In the darkness of space.

It is a blue and green marble
Placed in an unlit cupboard.

It is a shimmering gem
Lost in a dirty sheet.

It is an indigo and jade
Dropped in an instant blackout.

It is a turquoise lollipop
Lost in a dark cave.

It is a shiny bauble
Dropped in a gloomy puddle.

It is an azure and jade satellite
Lost in the darkness of space.

Bradley Tidball (9)
Ashcombe Primary School, Weston-super-Mare

What Is The Earth?

The Earth is a huge beach ball
Kicked up in the air, lost in a dark cave.

It is an enormous wave coming
Over a black house.

It is a giant football kicked up in the air,
In a dark room.

It is a blue piece of paper in a green cat's eye.

It is a blue top on a green piece of paper.

Joshua Harry Bell (10)
Ashcombe Primary School, Weston-super-Mare

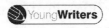

If I Was A Rocket

If I was a rocket
I would speed like a bullet
To a different galaxy.

If I was a rocket
I would zoom to Pluto
Like a fighter jet in the war.

If I was a rocket
I would play a game of dodgeball with the asteroids.

If I was a rocket
I would orbit the sun like a sleepy tornado.

If I was a rocket
I would visit the man on the moon
And take him a cake for tea.

**Alice Cullen, Emily Brimble, Daniel Hassell, Ben Lawrence,
Sophie Adams & Josh Bell (9 & 10)**
Ashcombe Primary School, Weston-super-Mare

What Is The Earth?

The Earth is a blob of mint ice cream
Lost in a pitch-black cave.

It is a giant light that shines bright
In a jet-black night sky.

It is a huge indigo and emerald football
Lost in a starless haunted house.

It is a round piece of jewellery that is silver and sparkly
With a black pillow in the background.

It is a pumpkin that has turned all green,
Dark in the sunless sky.

Lewis Street (10)
Ashcombe Primary School, Weston-super-Mare

What Is The Earth?

The Earth is like an azure eye
Staring out of the darkness of a cave.

It is like bubblegum and mint ice cream
Lost in a huge room of shadows.

It is an emerald and sapphire marble spinning round and round
Floating on a puddle of jet-black paint.

It is a round patch of blue sky with squirts of emerald paint
Spinning round on a giant's chalkboard.

It is a jade and sapphire gem
Lost in a dark black pair of curtains.

Jodie Filer (10)
Ashcombe Primary School, Weston-super-Mare

Limerick

There was once a boy called Jack
Who found a snake in his pack,
He cut it in two,
Gave half to the zoo
Then put the other half back!

Jessica Thiele (8)
Ashcombe Primary School, Weston-super-Mare

Henry VIII - Haiku

King Henry the VIII
Tudor King in history
Grumpy, mean and fat.

Lauren Small (9)
Ashcombe Primary School, Weston-super-Mare

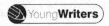

Rocket Poem

If I were a rocket
I'd zoom around the sun
And have a BBQ.

If I were a rocket
I'd fly around the solar system
And eat the galaxy.

If I were a rocket
I'd look at Saturn
And call it a doughnut.

If I were a rocket
I'd land in a crater on Mercury
And fill it with cola.

If I were a rocket
I'd fly in the sky
And find out if God was real.

Lachie Carver-Cox (9)
Ashcombe Primary School, Weston-super-Mare

The Perfect Present

Child catcher,
Face amazer,
Child surpriser,
Girl laughter.

Electricity waster,
Girly colour,
Bedroom filler,
Channel flicker!

Purple and pink telly.

Leah Chmielewski (9)
Ashcombe Primary School, Weston-super-Mare

The Rocket

If I were a rocket
I would spin around Earth
Like a whirlpool.

If I were a rocket
I would land on Pluto
And see my alien friends.

If I were a rocket
I would go to the sun and see it's a dot
And it's too hot.

If I were a rocket
I would blast into space
And eat all the stars.

If I were a rocket
I would fly around in space
And land on Neptune.

Jake Gale (9)
Ashcombe Primary School, Weston-super-Mare

The Rocket

If I were a rocket
I'd fly up to space to see Saturn
And fly around its rings.

If I were a rocket
I would go on Mars
And have a bit of Mars biscuit.

If I were a rocket
I would fly up to Jupiter
Because I am as big as him
And we can be friends.

If I were a rocket
I would play football with Pluto
And kick it around the universe.

Szymon Skorzak (9)
Ashcombe Primary School, Weston-super-Mare

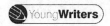

If I Were A Star

If I were a star
I would burn the planets.

If I were a star
I would glimmer like fire.

If I were a star
I would shine in the sky
Like a yellow ball kicked high into the sky.

If I were a star
I would skip to Mars to buy a Mars bar.

If I were a star
I would give the planets light.

If I were a star
I would play hide-and-seek with the planets.

Flynn Allier (10)
Ashcombe Primary School, Weston-super-Mare

The Alien Poem

The alien looks like a green, gooey monster.
He loves to eat animals.
His eyes are like eggs with black dots.
He has a very gross belly.
His teeth are shiny as metal.
He has red spots like chickenpox.
His feet are like crab claws.
He has antennae like a TV aerial.
He has an enormous head
But he is still my friend.

Umar Ali (10)
Ashcombe Primary School, Weston-super-Mare

The Rocket Poem

If I were a rocket
I would fly to the sun
To see shimmering light.

If I were a rocket
I would zigzag through the stars
To find the special three stars.

If I were an astronaut
I would try to discover
Something new.

If I were a rocket
I would try and make new friends
From outer space.

If I were a rocket
I would blast out of Earth
To Jupiter to discover a new planet.

Lottie Barnes (9)
Ashcombe Primary School, Weston-super-Mare

The Alien From Outer Space

The alien is funny.
He has a roomy overweight head.
The alien has a bulky belly.
His antennas are like TV antennas.
The teeth of the alien are as white as snow.
His eyes are like eggs with black dots in the middle.
His hands are like nuts.
His feet are like crab pinchers.
The alien lives on Mars and he is enormous.

Jack Williamson (9)
Ashcombe Primary School, Weston-super-Mare

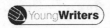
If I Were A Rocket

If I were a rocket
I would fly up high into space
And eat all the Galaxy bars.

If I were a spaceman
I would get into my space rocket
And go in marvellous space and ask an alien to be my best friend.

If I were a planet
I would spin our Earth round and round
Like a disco ball.

If I were a star
I would shine like the sun
And whizz off like a shooting star.

Kezie Sprague (9)
Ashcombe Primary School, Weston-super-Mare

My Best Journey

If I were a rocket
I would go to Mars and find a red alien
To be my friend.

If I were a rocket
I would go to Mercury and find a yellow alien
To be my friend.

If I were a rocket
I would go to Saturn and find a rainbow alien
To be my friend.

If I were a rocket
I would go back to Earth
And all the aliens I met would say, 'You're my friend!'

Caitlin Evans (10)
Ashcombe Primary School, Weston-super-Mare

The Alien

The alien's green and purple too
Its got eyes like shiny goo
And ears like elves, one red, one blue
It walks like a sea lion
With teeth like goo
Huge, chubby belly
Claws like crabs' snappers
His mouth is all slobbery and slimy like a snail trail
It has a long tongue with weird spots,
I think he has chickenpox.
He runs round like a maniac
But in the end he is my friend.

Harley Jay Spurling (10)
Ashcombe Primary School, Weston-super-Mare

The Freaky Alien

Enormous teeth like white, shiny, sharp metal
Spots like gigantic orange chickenpox
Feet like big green, creepy, terrifying crab claws

Tentacles like green, ugly, slithery, slimy, strange octopus
Eyes like three gone wrong rugby balls
Antennae like two zigzag aerials

Hands as green as a fully grown hedge
Tummy like an enormous purple overweight planet
Moves like a dizzy elephant

As scary as an alligator going crazy
As big as two giraffes
It was like a gigantic alien invasion.

Jordan Starling (9)
Ashcombe Primary School, Weston-super-Mare

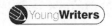

If I Were . . .

If I were a star
I would shine all day and night
And give some aliens some light.

If I were a rocket
I would blast into space
And find a new life form.

If I were an alien
I would squelch all around Pluto
And scare astronauts that invade my planet.

If I were the moon
I would look down at the people on Earth
And wonder what it is like to be one.

If I were anything else
I would miss being me!

Hannah Hollis Chilcott (10)
Ashcombe Primary School, Weston-super-Mare

The Alien

My alien has loads of muscles.
It is green.
It has spots like a football.
The shape of his ears are as round as Uranus or Mars.
It has two hands, a tentacle and a foot
And his favourite word is 'but'.
He likes to look around.
He also wants to be crowned.
He is 7 years old and is bald.
He slowly walks
And cannot talk.

Ty Jamieson (10)
Ashcombe Primary School, Weston-super-Mare

The Space Invader Poem

If I were a rocket
I would blast off into space
To find life on Mars

If I were a rocket
I would fly around the universe
And see if the moon is cheese

If I were a rocket
I would jump on a trampoline when my power is off
And try and reach the moon

If I were a rocket
I would race around Neptune
And tease it all day

If I were a rocket
I would see if Saturn is
As colourful as it says.

Lauren Filer (10)
Ashcombe Primary School, Weston-super-Mare

The Planets

In the air, out in space, it was quiet.
The planets were asleep,
Then they awoke and spun around like disco balls,
All different colours and shapes and sizes,
Stars and lights and lots of surprises.
While they dance around and play,
We can see the Milky Way.

Casey Walton (10)
Ashcombe Primary School, Weston-super-Mare

The Rocket

If I were a rocket
I would go to Jupiter
And put my face on it.

If I were a rocket
I would zoom into space
And explore the galaxy.

If I were a rocket
I would go to Mars
To buy a Mars bar.

If I were a rocket
I would blast off into space
And eat the stars.

Nathan Lammiman (9)
Ashcombe Primary School, Weston-super-Mare

The Mountain's Peak

Sands huddle together for shelter.
The lake lies still, all alone.
Trees slowly reach up to the stars with enthusiasm.
The beaming sun travels around the world glaring.
Leaves fall solemnly to the ground.
Waves leapfrog over the rocks in joy!
Dark shadows dance on the mountain's face.
The mountain stands tall and proud over the rocky shore.
Dust parts into the day.
The bark shrivels up old and wrinkly as the years pass.

Molly Turp (11)
Ashcombe Primary School, Weston-super-Mare

The Friendly Alien

The funny little critter
As crazy as can be
He laughs
As he bathes
He cares for baby bears
He has a whole head of hair!
He is orange, green, oh and purple too!
The friendly alien is getting tired now
So he gets inside his jar
If you're wondering why he has a jar
It's simply because
He lives on Mars!

Imogen Nicol (10)
Ashcombe Primary School, Weston-super-Mare

The Alien!

My alien is a funny one.
He has spots like chickenpox.
My alien's belly is enormous and
He eats big meals.

My alien has slippery, slimy, sticky
Legs like tentacles from an octopus.
My alien has got one yellow eye and
It is like a yellow rotten egg!

My alien's feet are like crab claws
My alien is a friendly alien
But most of all he's my friend!

Chloe Welfare (9)
Ashcombe Primary School, Weston-super-Mare

The Gas Giant

He's a gas giant
He's mighty
He's as strong as Captain Underpants
He has changed recently
An asteroid belt is between it and another planet
My mission is to find the planet

If I were to go round the gas giant
Meet its moons
Dine with aliens
It would just be perfect.

Adam Evans (10)
Ashcombe Primary School, Weston-super-Mare

The Alien

The alien is as chubby as a car
He is a bonkers, barmy alien
Three sticky fingers covered in mucus
He waddles in space like a penguin
Cracked eggy eyes
He has got Bugs Bunny's teeth
But he is my mate.

Bailey Syms (9)
Ashcombe Primary School, Weston-super-Mare

My Planet

If I were a planet
A spaceman would walk on me.

If I were a planet
A rocket would land on me.

If I were a planet
I would gaze at the other planets.

Hannah Jones (10)
Ashcombe Primary School, Weston-super-Mare

My Alien Poem

Spooky, spotty, slimy
Alley the alien is spotty, dotty like chickenpox.
He has goofy, shiny, sticky-out teeth
A cheesy smile like he is having a photo.
He has a red robin enormous tummy.
Feet like crab claws, spiky and sharp
Antennae zigzagged like aerials.
The humongous yellow egg eyes
Most of all he walks like a penguin.

Scarlett Fortune (10)
Ashcombe Primary School, Weston-super-Mare

The Mountain Scene

Shadows look longingly at the light that they cannot be in,
As the water sleeps still, in its bowl-like bed,
And the reflection stares up at the picture it is trying to paint,
The waves and the island battle wildly against each other,
All the bark holds on tightly to its tree, as the wind tries to pull it off,
The sand holds on helplessly to each other,
As the gentle waves pull it out to sea,
The soft clouds meander over the sky,
As if there are no worries in the world,
Leaves dance merrily to the beat of the wind,
That shouts at everything, as it whips by,
Rocks try to shield each other,
As mighty waves come crashing down on them,
The mountain proudly scans its surrounding area,
The sky looks down, amused at the Earth below it,
And the sun beams down upon the beautiful view below itself,
The mountain scene.

Lee Jennings (11)
Ashcombe Primary School, Weston-super-Mare

The Mountain Island

Leaves giggle with joy as they tickle each other.
Trees dance in the whispering wind.
The calm water shimmers in the daylight.
The mountain stands proud and tall.
Rocks rumble and tumble down the mountain hills.
The island awakes for a new day
As the sun shines like a thousand light bulbs.
Shadows twirl and dance in the light of the sun.

Lisa Williamson (10)
Ashcombe Primary School, Weston-super-Mare

The Open Nature

The island proudly looked around its perimeter,
Searching for new friends,
Shadows walk on the mountains to dance in the sun,
Currents in the sea swirl and dance in gentle harmony
With the sea creatures,
The sun views the Earth with a warm heart, staring at the continents,
The reflection stares back at itself
Thinking that the other one is his twin,
The wind blows the clouds which makes them sway with joy,
The sky watches the Earth below it, blowing strong winds for fun.
The mud giggles as some water rushes on to it,
Howling animals sing with the tweeting birds,
Making a soft gentle harmony.

Nathan Wilkins (10)
Ashcombe Primary School, Weston-super-Mare

The Mountain View

The mountain stares as the sun draws in,
Waves rush, jump and splash with joy,
Shadows walk swiftly in the wind,
The lake rests in peace as the night draws in,
The sun smiles as it hides away to sleep,
Up above the sky watches down on us,
Fluffy clouds walk slowly away into their beds,
Rocks moan as the waves come crashing on to them.

Erin Driscoll (10)
Ashcombe Primary School, Weston-super-Mare

Outstanding Nature

The mountain stands on its own proudly watching the life below.
The dust leaps and swirls in the air as it scatters everywhere.
The rocks moan as the sea comes crashing against them.
The lake glimmers and shines in the sun's rays.
The mud bathes in the sun listening to the birds.
Shadows run desperately, trying to get into the unreachable sun.
Clouds move around the sun and leave the Earth in total darkness.
The waves run to shore only to be dragged back into the murky depths.

Joe Withers (10)
Ashcombe Primary School, Weston-super-Mare

My Magic Box

(Based on 'Magic Box' by Kit Wright)

I will put in my box . . .
My very first deep breath next to my family.
My squealing voice crying my first word.
The amazing friends that I will never forget.
My first drop of blood. My never-ending heart.

I will put in my box . . .
The last flesh-puncturing gunshot of war.
The last slave to behold freedom.
The stinging whip of torture.
The bellowing roar of war -Something I could never imagine.

I will put in my box . . .
The 25th hour of the 13th month.
A white, fluffy sun and bright yellow clouds.
A devil honouring its heaven. God forbidding Hell.
A devil's pitiless footstep on the Earth.

My box is fashioned from
The first touch of glimmering gold
With the scent of dark Swiss chocolate.
Its hinges are made from dinosaur joints.
In its corners are little secrets never to be told.

I will go with my box to
The other side of the universe until I reach the end.
I will go to Hell and dig for the Earth's obliterating core.

But this is just a box
In my imagination - something I worship.

Christian Pickup (11)
Clayesmore Preparatory School, Blandford Forum

My Box Of Wishes

(Based on 'Magic Box' by Kit Wright)

I will put in my box . . .
The first teardrop shed at my birth,
The first 'hello' that echoed in my ears,
The first taste of baby milk,
The final *miaow* of PC, my cat,
The final goodbye of my nana.

I will put in my box . . .
A shimmering, shooting star,
A crescendo of musical notes,
The first crystal footprint on freshly fallen snow,
An elephant squirting water in the blazing desert heat,
Something called love.

I will put in my box . . .
My favourite woollen jumper,
My warm, snugly duvet with Squirty, my teddy, wrapped inside,
Poppies from the deepest meadow in France,
The constant tick of every second I live,
A sunset awaiting another beautiful day.

My box is fashioned from
Teeth from the tooth fairy's castle,
Silk and a red ribbon.

Its hinges are made from sparkling pearls,
And rainbow-coloured beads,
Its corners are filled with tiny boxes,
Each housing a memory.

I will go with my box to Hawaii,
To surf on an astonishing avalanche,
Not forgetting Aspen,
Where I will ski on a terrifying tidal wave.

Abi Morgan (11)
Clayesmore Preparatory School, Blandford Forum

Box Of Magic

(Based on 'Magic Box' by Kit Wright)

I will put in my box . . .
The last breath of eternal life,
A bite of melting chocolate,
A cloud enveloping a mountain,
The last tear shed on the Titanic,
And the first ray of sunshine.

I will put in my box . . .
The first steps of a young doe,
A sketching pencil to sketch the future,
An endless river that never reaches the sea,
The fall from the highest cliff to the deepest ocean,
An abandoned house where people lived, laughed,
Lingered and were lost.

I will put in my box . . .
The key to the universe,
The barrier that holds life from death,
The drop of sap from the tree that bore first life,
The first bud from the most beautiful rose
And the first song of the sweet nightingale.

My box is fashioned from
The beautiful oak wood that stretches
Up to the sky, gathering stars and dreams.

Its hinges are made from sirens' talons,
In its corners hides Death, waiting
To withdraw the lives of his victims.

I will go with my box to Saturn
To dance among the stars. Till the
Universe ends and all that is left is
My box.

Amelia Slay (11)
Clayesmore Preparatory School, Blandford Forum

My Magic Chest

(Based on 'Magic Box' by Kit Wright)

I will put in my box . . .
The hour-glass of my life,
Its hinges bone. My bone.
The memories of my ancestors
Frozen from life.
The scars of tyrants, whipping and whipping.
The burgers of Hell roasted on the flames.
The strawberries of Heaven preserved by love.

I will put in my box . . .
The last breath of Man.
The blue sky . . . the brown earth.
The warmth of a pet.
Death's scythe - pure darkness.

I will put in my box . . .
A golden drachma to
Pay my way.
A child's limp bone.
The Lord's Cross.
God's wrath to Hell's locals.

My box is fashioned from
A hide of darkness,
A frozen memory.
Its hinges are made from pure light,
God's light bulb.
In its corners sing a choir of angels.

I will go with my box to the palace of the Soul.
The court of God.
Hell's void.

Home.

Sam Christmas (10)
Clayesmore Preparatory School, Blandford Forum

My Box Of Me

(Based on 'Magic Box' by Kit Wright)

I will put in my box . . .
The piano of Tim Minchin,
The sweet taste of roast chicken,
The last sunset on Earth,
The last story ever told,
A beaming ray of the sun.

I will put in my box . . .
The sound of nature's song,
The smell of my favourite meal,
The hair of Medusa,
The hat of Michael Jackson,
The first rainbow ever created.

I will put in my box . . .
The memories of my first day of school -
Good and bad!
The victory of the Second World War
The wig of Queen Elizabeth the 1st,
A unicorn's horn.

My box is fashioned from
The wings of angels,
Covered in silky feathers
The way God made them.
Its hinges are made from the shining light of the moon.
In its corners are the lives of people who died in battle.

I will go with my box to live on the planet Mars,
Where I could float effortlessly in mid-air,
Then I would climb a volcano.

Theo Fraser (11)
Clayesmore Preparatory School, Blandford Forum

My Box

(Based on 'Magic Box' by Kit Wright)

I will put in my box . . .
The first shimmering snowdrop in summer,
The gleaming scythe that massacred Kronos,
My first smile that washed across my face,
And happiness.

I will put in my box . . .
The black destruction of war,
The tortured pain of those who fight,
The cessation of my heart,
The last spark of life in the universe,
And the soul of me - trapped in its deepest black hole.

I will put in my box . . .
The last croaking gasp of a snake dying,
Poison of a mother's never-ending kiss,
The burning hatred of a jealous brother.
The cold, black sun that gleams across the sky.
The feeling that a mother experiences
When her children are lost.

My box is fashioned from . . .
The ashes of our sun
And the final, dying embers of humanity as it faces
The endless crush of the universe.
Its hinges are made from the scales of the Hydra.
In it are jokes of a clown.

I will go with my box to the end,
To the last cry of an eagle
And face the Kraken in the last moments.

Will Christmas (10)
Clayesmore Preparatory School, Blandford Forum

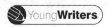

My Magic Box

(Based on 'Magic Box' by Kit Wright)

I will put in my box . . .
The roar of a racing car zooming by,
A yellow moon and a silver sun,
The 13th month covered with dust from silver stars,
The first step of life and the sprint towards death,
The first breath and the final scream.

I will put in my box . . .
The weirdness of normal and the emptiness of strange,
A light from darkness and the darkness of light,
A step towards life and a step towards death,
Me being given birth,
A sight I've never seen.

I will put in my box . . .
A heart-ripping battle and the joy of peace,
The creation of the world and life-ending explosions,
A burning light with comforting darkness,
A trickle of a waterfall and the gushing of a stream,
A sea of blood with sinking ships.

My box is fashioned from
Ice taken from Mt Everest
With metamorphic rock from Mt Vesuvius.
It grips golden treasure from the Titanic,
Its hinges are made from the
Tusks of elephants,
In its corners I will hide my deepest secrets with a golden cloth.

I will go with my box to the nine wonders of the world,
I will fly there on a surfboard and surf on a wing.

Ashish Thapa (10)
Clayesmore Preparatory School, Blandford Forum

Magic Box

(Based on 'Magic Box' by Kit Wright)

I will put in my box . . .
The silent stars that linger above me,
The magic of my last fable,
The azure water of a clear spring,
The mountain that you can't climb,
The light of the yellow moon.

I will put in my box . . .
The first fragrance of spring,
The last catamaran to sail the North Sea,
The last train to leave Mars,
The 25 hour clock,
The first sight of the winter sun.

I will put in my box . . .
The last snowfall on Jupiter,
The plume of a young pheasant,
The first mist of a summer morning,
The unlucky horseshoe,
The day that never starts.

My box is fashioned from . . .
The sensitive feathers from an ostrich,
And it is lined with the finest vicuna.

Its hinges are made from the rarest ivory.

In its corners are the secrets of the wild ocean.

I will go with my box to the peak of the Earth
And then sail the Red Sea
Into the evening sun.

Olivia Farrant (10)
Clayesmore Preparatory School, Blandford Forum

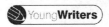

My Magic Box

(Based on 'Magic Box' by Kit Wright)

I will put in my box . . .
The cheers of my last match when I scored a goal,
The buzz of a bee on a winter afternoon.
The last conversation with my mum.
The awkward silence at a family reunion.
The petrified look on my brother's face when I scare him.

I will put in my box . . .
The last taste of sweet summer fruit,
The darkness of a flower,
The lightness of night,
The last excruciating punch in a boxing match.
The last green leaf in autumn.

I will put in my box . . .
The elephant my gran got me from Thailand,
The A* I got for my history project,
The last snowflake in winter,
The first ray of sunlight in spring,
And the first drops of melted snow.

My box is fashioned from
The hottest fire and the coldest water.

Its hinges are made from silver, bronze and gold.
In its corners hide little white lies.

I will go with my box to Jamaica to sunbathe
In the snow
Then I will go to Antarctica to
Shop on the ice.

Asia Jones (10)
Clayesmore Preparatory School, Blandford Forum

My Magic Box

(Based on 'Magic Box' by Kit Wright)

I will put in my box . . .
The thirteenth month
Winnie the Pooh's honey,
An ogre in a house,
A businessman in a swamp,
Luigi's green hat.

I will put in my box . . .
Fresh blood from a beating heart,
Voldemort's snake,
Stephen Hawkin's wheelchair
The evil of an angel,
The sacredness of Satan.

I will put in my box . . .
The first raindrop of autumn,
The Simpsons' television,
The first rugby ball ever made,
The great glass elevator
And James' giant peach.

My box is fashioned from
Steel and Einstein's blood
With a shooting star on the lid.
Its hinges are made from the Devil's horns,
In its corners are the victims the sickle has killed.

I will go with my box to Gallifrey
And hide in a deep hole dug by Beethoven,
I will travel there by a flying boat
With big sails and a lookout point.

Rory Highnam (10)
Clayesmore Preparatory School, Blandford Forum

My Magic Box

(Based on 'Magic Box' by Kit Wright)

I will put in my box . . .
A single teardrop from my mother and father,
The pearly shine of my brother's white teeth,
Final wheezing laughs from the last of my grandparents,
Shooting stars I never saw.
Constant ticks of life's clock.

I will put in my box . . .
Icy spray from the depths of Niagara Falls,
The cage in which my memories are kept,
The tip of the Eiffel Tower.
Silky sand from the Sahara,
A trickle of water from the Pacific.

I will put in my box . . .
A tiny piece of stuffing
From each of my two most loved teddies,
My duvet cover that wraps around me,
The number 93.
All of my milk teeth,
My steamy breath on a cold day,
My first smile when I have my braces off.

My box is fashioned from
Gleaming pearls and dry ice
So cold you can see the steam rising.
Its hinges are made from real silver, patterned with amber,
In its corners float cloud formations.

I will go with my box through countryside and valleys,
Past the place where no one goes,
Through the stars,
Into nothing . . .
And back again.

Ellie Beckett (11)
Clayesmore Preparatory School, Blandford Forum

Viking Raiders

The ferocious pirates
Use their strength to
Pull up their oak boat.
They blow their curved, evil, wooden horn.
It is as loud as a vicious lion's roar.
Fierce Vikings run as fast as the cold
Evening wind can take them
With their deadly weapons, they raid!
People hear them
Roar and shout at the top of their voices
Killing the monks
Who fall down in pain
Small huts are raided
Vikings only want golden jewels and crops
From the poor Anglo Saxons
Vikings smash through doors
People can't hide!
They're like bulls charging!
After the pirates run back to the longship
And face the terrifying seas!

Bethany Wadley (11)
East Huntspill Primary School, East Huntspill

Viking Raiders

Sneaky, terrifying warriors with their deadly weapons
Charge and jump into the fast longship
Rowing off
Raiding for gold and glistening jewels.

They take their sharp axes, swords and shields.
Their weapons are covered in blood.
Anglo-Saxons scream
Violent Vikings steal and murder!

Harry Elsworth (8)
East Huntspill Primary School, East Huntspill

Viking Raiders

Vicious, violent Vikings
Getting ready for their big raid packing
Swords, axes, shields and helmets
Into the strong longships
In the sparkling sun
Fearless Vikings jumping into the magnificent
Longships one by one sitting down on sea chests
Starting to row along the calm rivers.

Ferocious Vikings grabbing their blood-coloured axes
Running out of the longships hiding behind the banks
Of Anglo-Saxons
Evil, sneaky Vikings running as fast as cheetahs to attack
The Anglo-Saxons and get their treasured jewels and maids
They fight for hours and hours without stopping
Their swords are covered in dark red blood
Dripping on the ground
As they walk back to the longship.

Shannon Hooper (9)
East Huntspill Primary School, East Huntspill

The Sea Explorers

Terrifying warriors get ready
Sailing off to calm, hardworking England
Stealing viciously across the land.
They get ready their terrifying, attacking weapons,
They travel quickly across the heaving, hard sea!
The ferocious Vikings creep up behind rocks.
Jump out at people in the quiet village.
Stealing lots of gold, silver plates, killing lots of people.
Taking poor slaves back to Scandinavia.

Katie Miller (10)
East Huntspill Primary School, East Huntspill

Viking

A beautiful longship,
Moves like a crocodile
Through the water
Coming out of the sea
Like a zombie!

Vikings running to the Saxon villages,
Like cheetahs
Raiding like charging rhinos.

Viking swords shining like deadly diamonds
Killing people with them!

Jack Priddice (10)
East Huntspill Primary School, East Huntspill

Vikings

Fierce invaders
Pack their evil weapons
Axes, swords, shields and helmets
Into a scary, hand-made oak longship.

Women weave huge sails
These are pulled up and tied
Vikings set sail in their precious longship
Like sneaky mice.

They land
They jump out fast and shout!
Anglo-Saxons scream
Everything goes silent . . .

Stealing treasure and jewels
Raiding again and again
Eventually they will settle.

Matthew Phillips (8)
East Huntspill Primary School, East Huntspill

Viking Raider

Evil, terrifying warriors
Pack their sea chests with deadly weapons
Axes, swords and shields for the raid
Warriors take food for the long journey.

The scary oak longship
Is like a dragon breathing fire
As scary as a sea monster
Sleek and very fast!

Warriors bring back slaves
Gold and jewels
Settlers too as well as raiders.

Joe Priddice (8)
East Huntspill Primary School, East Huntspill

Viking Raiders

Terrifying scary Vikings
Packed the deadly weapons into their carved, oak,
Strong, monster longship.
Raiding the Anglo-Saxon
With blood-stained ferocious axes, swords
And other warrior tools.

The bloodthirsty Vikings
Jumping in and out of their monster longship.
Raiding places, Vikings stealing
Anglo-Saxons to be the Viking slaves.

Bradley Huett (9)
East Huntspill Primary School, East Huntspill

Viking Raiders

Scary Vikings
Setting off for a vicious raid.
Raiding for hard gold and shimmering jewels.
Hiding deep in their magnificent longship.
Raiding tools, gruesome axes and swords.

Rebekah Fey (7)
East Huntspill Primary School, East Huntspill

Vikings

Gruesome, ground-shaking Vikings
Slaughtering all that's in their way
Ground as red as fiery lava
Terrifying black smoke
Screams fill the air.

Joel Thomas (9)
East Huntspill Primary School, East Huntspill

Viking Raiders

At sunrise Viking warriors load their mighty longship
Putting strong metal weapons into the dragon-headed longship.

They set off on the stormy sea raiding Britain!
To steal and take over.
Taking anything they find.

Vikings raid the terrified Anglo-Saxons
Taking treasures and sad slaves.

Ruby Peters (7)
East Huntspill Primary School, East Huntspill

Viking Raiders

Rowing, sailing through the night and day
Moving on to their fight
Over the glowing seas in little time
Finding out what lands are about.

Sleek, mighty, glorious things
Move swiftly and silently
Doing their thing
Evil, terrifying raiding boats,
Sail around looking the most deadly
Scary, spooky and violent weapons
Are carried around like family memories.

Sneaking up to the Anglo-Saxons
Scaring them to their highest point
'Charge!' the Vikings will shout
Making everyone want to move out.

Ellie-May Venn (9)
East Huntspill Primary School, East Huntspill

Planets

Melting Mercury is a small fireball, hot like lava,
Vibrating Venus is the second to the Sun,
Enormous Earth is the third closest to the Sun with lots of shining colours,
Magnificent Mars is a mini planet like a golf ball
And its nickname is the Red Planet,
Joyful Jupiter is the greatest of all and has many moons,
Super Saturn has a multitude of rings,
Unusual Uranus is as green as green,
Nautical Neptune is the 8th away from the Sun,
Poor Pluto is the smallest of all and is a floating ice cube.

Joseph Allen (8)
Horsington CE (VA) Primary School, Templecombe

Meet The Aliens

Amazing aliens zooming around space
In their flying saucers
Landing on the dark side of the moon,
Dust is everywhere,
Travelling on towards Earth.
Landing on a concrete road - scanning!
People shouting and screaming
Returning to Mars.

Ciarán Reynolds (7)
Horsington CE (VA) Primary School, Templecombe

The Cold Moon

The cold moon is covered in craters,
The cold moon is grey like a ball,
The cold moon is round like a ball,
The cold moon is playing hide-and-seek,
The cold moon is smaller than Earth.

Georgia Chant (8)
Horsington CE (VA) Primary School, Templecombe

Planets

Mini Mercury, like melting lava,
Vibrant Venus, second closest to the boiling sun, full of energy,
Elegant Earth, all blue and green,
Mars is the fourth planet like a big tomato,
Jolly Jupiter like a massive orange sweet,
Super Saturn has many moons,
Unsteady Uranus, many light years away,
Naughty Neptune, blue all over,
Pluto, all alone right at the back, now a dwarf,
Not forgetting our massive Moon with many craters.

Kieran Burpitt (8)
Horsington CE (VA) Primary School, Templecombe

Shimmering Space

Space is as shiny as glittering glass,
Her stars are as beautiful as fine dance dresses,
Rockets flying through splendid space with furious fire,
Sparkly, shimmery metal,
Carrying famous and brave astronauts
Through the Milky Way,
Craters feel like they're racing past like the Olympic Games
With the fastest star racers.
Astronauts whizzed past Mars
At such a pace it's a blur.
Fabulous fun is found with the human race.

Madeleine Astill (8)
Horsington CE (VA) Primary School, Templecombe

Planets

Mini Mercury, the hottest around, so close to the sun,
Burning Venus, hot in the day and cold at night,
Enormous Earth with water, land and children play,
The moon, a big sphere, like a giant football with large holes inside it,
Molten Mars, a very spotty planet,
Jolly Jupiter, the largest of them all with many spinning moons,
Swirling Saturn, the yellow planet, like a lemon,
Unusual Uranus, it's so green, like a lime,
Naughty Neptune, the gassiest planet, like a big blueberry,
Funny Pluto, the smallest planet, like a dot,
And finally the sun, 5538 degrees, like a mango!

Joshua Nancarrow (8)
Horsington CE (VA) Primary School, Templecombe

The Planets

The huge planets shine brightly,
As they travel round glistening outer space,
Murky Mercury, so hot it might blow blood,
Violent Venus covered with speckly red spots,
Living Earth, the blue and green lovely colours,
Mad Mars, as red as blood,
Gigantic Jupiter is the largest planet,
Unusual Uranus, greener than grass,
Nipping Neptune, a sea of blue,
Shining sun, her lovely bright light gives us life.

Rosie Ratcliffe (7)
Horsington CE (VA) Primary School, Templecombe

Starry Space

Shining stars are turning, whooshing and whirling,
Shooting stars are swirling swiftly around gloomy space,
I soar up high,
I wonder why golden stars are turning in the deep black sky so high,
Silver moon, a jewel on its own,
How it sparkles in the dark inky sky,
Night is pitch-black but the glittering stars are bright,
So I wonder why the dazzling stars in the sky twinkle down on me,
I wish I could be a glossy star,
I hope they live there, so beautiful in the night.

Jessica Deverell (8)
Horsington CE (VA) Primary School, Templecombe

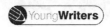

Bug Bird's Planet

Bug Bird is one of my many friends,
Bug Bird's story never ends.
Into never-ending space,
Bug Bird pulls a funny face.

Now little Bug Bird will travel the universe for us to see:
Boiling hot Mercury is closest to the blazing sun,
Vecod Venus is second, gosh it's numb,
Rounded Earth has one rocky moon, people will be living on it soon,
Marvellous Mars has many shooting stars,
Jumping Jupiter with its arched rings,
Bug Bird's never seen as many things,
Swirling Saturn with whizzing rings,
Small Uranus is like an ice ball,
Tiny Neptune and Pluto are the coldest of all.

So here Bug Bird is at the end of space,
Floating away from the human race!

Amber Mary Wright (8)
Horsington CE (VA) Primary School, Templecombe

Mars

Marvellous Mars is red like blood,
Martians running and playing games,
Looking at the galaxy,
Tiny Pluto, a dwarf planet,
Giant Jupiter and Saturn,
Little Martians off to blue Earth,
Moon's many craters,
Shining white when the day is gone.
Darkness grows when the night arrives,
The stars shine brightly,
All asleep, even on the space station,
Out of control, returning to space.

Polly Davis (7)
Horsington CE (VA) Primary School, Templecombe

Extraterrestrial

The remote aliens have a sticky smell,
The aliens are coming because they want our Earth,
The antagonistic aliens flying in rockets past the moon,
Blasting through space,
Aliens watching everything,
Landing using their super fast rockets.

Charlie Osborne (9)
Horsington CE (VA) Primary School, Templecombe

The Little Green Men

Staring from my window one night I saw a green frisbee,
I put on my soft slippers and rushed outside into the darkness,
The frisbee shook and so did I,
So I ran inside,
A tiny door opened in the frisbee,
A squad of men stepped outside,
Green all over,
They asked me in for a cup of Martian tea,
I brought home-made cakes,
They said, 'Goodbye,'
And left for Mars!

Alice Macey (7)
Horsington CE (VA) Primary School, Templecombe

Wonderful Space

Outstanding space is fantastic,
Glittering stars in the galaxy,
Rocky Mars,
Amazing asteroids searching for the giant moon,
Stars gleaming,
Green aliens out in the dark,
Silver astronauts on space walks,
All this happens whilst on Earth we sleep!

Joseph Gartell (7)
Horsington CE (VA) Primary School, Templecombe

Planets

Ten,
Nine,
Eight,
Seven,
Six,
Five,
Four,
Three,
Two,
One,
Blast-off!
Off to Mercury, it's like melting lava,
Off to Venus, that is like a stripy zebra,
Off to Mars to see shooting stars,
Off to Jupiter to see its red spot,
Off to Saturn to see the rings,
Off to Neptune to see its blueness,
Off to Pluto, it's the smallest,
Back to Earth to see our human family!

Imogen Morris (8)
Horsington CE (VA) Primary School, Templecombe

Planets

Mini Mercury is as blazing as melting lava,
Venus is as stripy as a zebra,
Earth is as blue as the deep blue sea,
The moon is like a shiny disco ball.
Could there be Martians on Mars?
Jumping Jupiter has sixteen spinning moons,
Saturn is as colourful as a clownfish,
Uranus is as green as grass,
Neptune is as blue as a blueberry.

Luke Brewer (9)
Horsington CE (VA) Primary School, Templecombe

The Rocket

The rocket is shiny,
The rocket is red,
The rocket looks like it's on fire,
The rocket is flashy.

Becky Osborne (8)
Horsington CE (VA) Primary School, Templecombe

Planets

There are thousands, millions or billions of different shining stars,
Boiling Mercury is the closest planet to the sun,
Tiny Earth is the third planet to the sun,
We live on the fantastic Earth,
God made the fantastic Earth,
The moon has craters
And there are lonely flags on its crust,
Mars is a pinky colour, not like the chocolate bars.
Neptune is blue like a misty blue ice.

Rosie Cotterell (7)
Horsington CE (VA) Primary School, Templecombe

Planets

Mercury is like a golden medal,
Venus is like a golden sun,
Mars is like a rosy, ripe apple
Jupiter has a tiny red Smartie,
Saturn has rings like coins,
Neptune is like a blue sky,
The moon is like a silver globe,
Earth is like a colourful football.

Sophie Shave (7)
Horsington CE (VA) Primary School, Templecombe

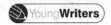

Life In Space

Space is wonderful,
Gloomy stars,
Shining planets,
Endless asteroids and the guiding North Star.
The biggest star in our solar system,
Is the sun, a ball of gas.
Muted Mercury,
Vented Venus,
Endless Earth,
Moulded Mars,
Jumping Jupiter,
Salted Saturn,
Useful Uranus,
Noble Neptune
And finally playful Pluto.

Michael Tarling (8)
Horsington CE (VA) Primary School, Templecombe

Perfect Planets

There are nine planets in our solar system,
All the planets have extraordinary colours,
Earth is like light creamy blue,
Neptune is as bright as the blue sea,
Mars is as ripe as a bright red apple,
Saturn has a bright golden ring,
Jupiter is a juicy bright colour,
Venus is like the golden sun,
Mercury is like a golden medal.

Sophie Gartell (9)
Horsington CE (VA) Primary School, Templecombe

Shimmering Space

The shimmering space like the beautiful still water on epic Earth,
The spiky sun, one glimpse and your eyes will water,
Misty moon that caught your eye like a baby bear,
Epic Earth, the colourful greens and blues like the colourful picture.
Magical Mars is perfect red and it almost looks like it's dead,
Juicy Jupiter is the largest planet in our solar system,
Shiny Saturn the yellow and orange drag your eyes towards the colour,
Nippy Neptune rings like a dull rainbow.

Sarah Maunsell (8)
Horsington CE (VA) Primary School, Templecombe

Planets

There is nine planets in our solar system,
Marvellous Mercury closest to the sun,
Venus has no rings,
Earth is the planet we live on,
Mars is one of the closest planets to Earth,
Jupiter has sixteen moons,
Saturn is a gas planet,
Uranus has a ring,
Neptune only moves slowly around the sun.

Henry Lambert (8)
Horsington CE (VA) Primary School, Templecombe

Planets

The steaming sun is boiling hot like white flames burning your skin,
Minnie Mercury, tiny compared to the sun and is the first planet,
Vicious Venus is the second planet in the solar system,
The moon is as white as a shepherd and as grey as a snowstorm,
Earth is round and is the third planet in the solar system,
Amazing Mars, as red as a strawberry and is the fourth planet,
Jumping Jupiter, multicoloured and is the fifth planet,
Smart Saturn is orange and a yellowed-brown and is the sixth planet,
Useful Uranus is green all over it, made of gas and is the seventh planet,
Second last is nice Neptune, blue all over it and is the eighth planet.

Holly Gilbert-Eastwood (7)
Horsington CE (VA) Primary School, Templecombe

Mad, Bad Chad

There once was a young boy called Chad
Whose ideas were incredibly bad
He tripped up his nan
Hit his dad with a pan
And made his mum terribly sad.

Rachel Knight (10)
Lancaster House School, Weston-super-Mare

My Dog Moses

Moses is black
Likes chasing the cat.
The cats has no choice,
When he makes such a noise.
He runs straight up the tree,
But Moses can see
The cat stalking a bird.
Woof! Miaow! Squawk! Oh my word!

Phillipa Hooper (10)
Lancaster House School, Weston-super-Mare

My Strange Pets

My birds wear a hat,
My dog wears a dress,
My guinea pig wears a cap every day.
My ponies wear a vest,
When they do a sky-diving test,
My hamsters go shopping in Gap.
My cat's chest is full of money
For the hamster to spend.
My mouse nibbles his toes
While my snail blows his nose.
My dog wears a tutu
And likes doing Sudoku.

Lucie Bouchere-Roseff (9)
Lancaster House School, Weston-super-Mare

Rainbow

R ain and sun are how it's made
A dded together, a magical blend.
I love the colours of every shade
N o one has ever found the end
B ending and stretching across the sky,
O ver the fields or in the city;
W ish you could stay, my shining friend,
　　You're fading now - what a pity!

Milla O'Meara (9)
Lancaster House School, Weston-super-Mare

Easter

E gg hunting
A round the garden
S hining eggs hidden in the leaves
T ime for fun
E ating chocolate is allowed
R ules relaxed - for Easter.

Georgie Midgley (9)
Lancaster House School, Weston-super-Mare

My Mum

My mum is like a cute hamster
Because she likes to keep to herself

My dad is like a cavernous giraffe
Because he is really tall

My brother is like a small rat
Because he is very small

My grandmother is like a nice cute puppy
Because she is a very nice person.

Joshua Walker (9)
Long Cross Primary & Nursery School, Bristol

On The Way To School

On the way to school I saw a rat
Running along the road
It was a grey-coloured rat
It was a fierce, grey-coloured rat
It was a round, fierce, grey-coloured rat
It was an old, round, fierce, grey-coloured rat
It was a falling over, old, round, fierce, grey-coloured rat
And it got ran over by a car.

Jake Buckle (9)
Long Cross Primary & Nursery School, Bristol

My Brother Is Like A . . .

My older brother is like a dog
Because he shouts a lot.

My younger brother is like a mouse
Because he doesn't speak much.

My big sister is like a teacher
Because she bosses everyone around!

Eli Hunt (9)
Long Cross Primary & Nursery School, Bristol

My Mum Is A . . .

My mum is a hairy monkey,
When she gets out of bed.

My dad is an angry dog,
When I don't do as I'm told.

My brother is like a sneaky snake,
When he comes in my room and steals things.

My sister is a greedy pig,
Because she eats a lot.

Abbey McGill (9)
Long Cross Primary & Nursery School, Bristol

On The Way To The Rainforest

I saw a jaguar
It was an orange jaguar
It was a spotty, orange jaguar
It was a scary, spotty, orange jaguar
And it was scared of me!

Brooke Alison Leanne Williams (10)
Long Cross Primary & Nursery School, Bristol

Titanic

Steam maker
People carrier
Lifeboat saver
Iceberg breaker
Bell ringer
Ship sinker.

Charles Pearce (8)
Manor Court Community Primary School, Chard

My Dog

Face licker
Silent hunter
Fast runner
Scruffy fur
Messy eater
Tail wagger
Hole digger
Bone chewer
Loud howler
Big cuddler
Children lover!

Alice Mabel Peacock (8)
Manor Court Community Primary School, Chard

My Hamster

Little nipper
Claw biter
Sock snuggler
Finger ripper
Nestbox maker
Fab hider
Lettuce eater
Fantastic comforter
Good racer
Small rodent
Milk drinker
Big stinker.

Abigail Jessopp (8)
Manor Court Community Primary School, Chard

My Baby Sister

A cry one
A happy one
A cutie one
A noisy one
A lazy one
A hungry one
A kisser one
A cuddler one
A mummy one
My one.

Kirsty Hooper (8)
Manor Court Community Primary School, Chard

My Dog

Messy eater
Ball chaser
Cat scarer
Loud barker
Biscuit eater
Teddy nipper
Good cricketer
Bone chewer.

Jack Turner (8)
Manor Court Community Primary School, Chard

My Husky

Barking skiller
Meat ripper
Really loud barker
Really bad farter
Really bad digger
Really good runner
A bear snipper
A river sipper.

Joshua Davies (8)
Manor Court Community Primary School, Chard

My Husky

Snowy white
He won't bite
Howler, growler
Meat eater
Cute sleeper
But such a snorer
Taking parter
Bad farter!

Chloe Nicole Teague (8)
Manor Court Community Primary School, Chard

Mum

Hard worker
Old lady carer
Clothes washer
Heavy sleeper
Great cooker
Tea lover
Brilliant drawer.

Damian Hall (8)
Manor Court Community Primary School, Chard

Monkey

Banana eater
Tree climber
Noise maker
Excellent swinger
Brilliant gymnast
Super sleeper.

Chloe Murray (7)
Manor Court Community Primary School, Chard

My Cat

Outdoor lover
Mouse chaser
Bed sleeper
Fast eater
Fantastic climber
Quick drinker.

Paul Rowe (7)
Manor Court Community Primary School, Chard

Murderous Midnight

Thumping feet
Crunch in the snow.

Eyes are red as a ruby
Teeth are like razor blades.

Fingernails have a poisonous touch
Toenails are like daggers.

The huge black beast creeps in the dark
Invisible in the night.

Roaring like a million lions
While tensing his muscles.

Beware of wandering at midnight
You just might be struck
By a poisonous claw.

Oliver Houghton (9)
Marksbury Primary School, Bath

My Friends

I like my friends, there's six of us
And we always stick together.
When the big bad things come we stay hand in hand
They look after me and I look after them
Like we always do.

When we break up we always come back together again,
We play lots of games at lunch, it is very fun
We've each got different personalities but we go together well.
I like my friends, there's six of us
And we always stick together.

Jessica Hill (9)
Marksbury Primary School, Bath

Seasons

Winter
In the winter I stare out the steamy window
To see white blankets of crystallised snow,
Where a snowman will lie.
Children run about with rosy cheeks till the eve of the day.

Spring
In spring the juicy buttercups and daffodils
Peep up between the fresh green grass.
On the bank I watch the cool water trickle
Down the rocks.

Summer
In the summer the sun beats down on the bright yellow sunflowers,
Filling the air with joy.
Children run about laughing and playing,
Adults lounge in the sun reading or just sleeping.

Autumn
In autumn the blue heavens begin to float away
And the sky is filled with a hazy, grey mist.
The leaves scrunch up and then one by one fall
Off the trees and begin to dart through the wind,
Weaving in and out the towering trees.

Charlotte Scruton (9)
Marksbury Primary School, Bath

Evacuation

Anxious as I wait in the crooked old train station.
My name tag hung around my weak neck.
The gas mask at the ready in a little wooden box,
The sound of people crying fills my eyes with water.
The train appears out of nowhere,
Thundering down the track.
My suitcase is in my hand, all ready and packed.
Tears stream down my face as the train pulls away,
I hope I see London once again.

Maisie Humphries (9)
Marksbury Primary School, Bath

My Christmas Senses

I can hear people laughing with joy,
Opening presents and playing with toys!
Bells ringing, people rushing to church with a bound,
Children hopping over the snow-white mounds.

I can see huge carpets of snow lying around the church
And red robins sitting on their perch.
As I slouch in front of the welcoming fire,
Watching the mince pies as they sleep.

I can smell the roast turkey in the oven,
Sizzling and I like to watch Mum,
Making gravy for drizzling,
Like raindrops in the autumn on a dark day.
The smell of scented candles fill the room
Like the smell of lilies in May.

Meg Stratton (8)
Marksbury Primary School, Bath

Evacuees

E scaping to the countryside
V ery scary
A way from Mum and Dad
C an you come?
U pset kids all around
A wfully sad
T emporary new homes
I n the train, on our way
O ut of the way of bombs
N ow we are safe.

George Lippiatt (8)
Marksbury Primary School, Bath

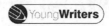

My Uncle

My uncle is very strong.
My uncle works all day long.

My uncle carves things from wood.
My uncle does things I wish I could.

My uncle makes me laugh aloud.
My uncle makes funny sounds.

My uncle is special and very kind.
My uncle is often on my mind.

I love my uncle.

Katie Vockings (8)
Marksbury Primary School, Bath

Summer

When the sun is shining bright,
People come out to play.
To holiday, swimming pool,
To a beach far away.
Hosepipes and water guns,
A water fight they will make.
Coca-Cola, cherryade and
Fruit to make a shake.
Flowers blooming in the garden,
Looking very nice.
Families having barbecues,
With lots of spicy rice!

Tayla Lye-Taylor (9)
Marksbury Primary School, Bath

World War II Acrostic Poem

E vacuees journey
V ery frightened
A nxious children
C rying deeply
U nbelievable things happening
A ngry but understanding why
T rain journey to somewhere new
I t's scary for those children
O nward bound to their hosts
N o one knows if they will go back.

Tazmin Blows (8)
Marksbury Primary School, Bath

What Am I?

I am a fluffy creature,
With a wet nose, pointy ears and soft paws,
I am as cute as a hamster,
I am very hairy,
With light fur,
Long flaky whiskers
And teeth as sharp as knives.
What am I?

A: A cat.

Joshua Weatherstone (7)
Mendip Green First School, Weston-super-Mare

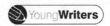

My Monkey

I have a pet monkey
And Charlie is his name
And throwing coconuts is his favourite game.
I have a pet monkey
He likes to joke around
He should have a red nose
As he is like a clown.
I have a pet monkey
I sleep with him at night
He keeps me warm and cosy
And I hold him nice and tight.

Sian Carroll (7)
Mendip Green First School, Weston-super-Mare

What Am I?

I am grey and big
I eat peanuts.
I have massive ears.
I have a short tail that is like a pencil.
I have a big trunk.
I am bigger than a rhino.
I have big eyes.
I smell like peanuts.
I feel bumpy all over.
What am I?

A: An elephant.

Grace Clifford (8)
Mendip Green First School, Weston-super-Mare

What Am I?

I am very vicious,
I creep around in your garden,
I am ginger,
I like to eat chickens when I am angry,
I do not make a sound,
I move super fast,
I smell like a chicken,
I go wild when I see a human.
What am I?

A: A fox.

Daisy Freeman (7)
Mendip Green First School, Weston-super-Mare

What Am I?

I come out at night,
With big staring eyes,
My pointy beak ready for a treat.
I eat small animals and sometimes even fish.
My small feathery wings help me fly silently,
And my talons are as sharp as knives.

What am I?

A: An owl.

Nicholas Robinson (7)
Mendip Green First School, Weston-super-Mare

What Am I?

I am blue.
I have sharp teeth.
I have a triangle on my back.
I have red blood on my teeth.
I have rough meat to eat.
I live in the deep blue sea.
I have fishy friends.
I have black eyes.

Who am I?

A: A shark.

Riley Staddon (8)
Mendip Green First School, Weston-super-Mare

What Am I?

I have a big furry mane.
I have a big roar.
I am very big.
I can run as fast as a cheetah.
What am I?

A: A lion.

Libby Moss (7)
Mendip Green First School, Weston-super-Mare

What Am I?

I run like a cheetah, very, very fast
I have stripes on my back
In a race I don't come last
I am orange and black with stripes on my back.
What am I?

A: A tiger.

Courtney Ellis (7)
Mendip Green First School, Weston-super-Mare

Fright

I have a fin as pointy as can be
I'm the fast speedy fish in the sea
So you can't catch me.
My teeth are like daggers
Ready to bite.
I will give you such a fright
I'm a shark.

Devon Crabb (8)
Mendip Green First School, Weston-super-Mare

What Am I?

I am yellow with brown spots.
My neck is long like a tree trunk.
I eat from trees.
My tail is long and thin like a piece of string.
I have black hooves
And big eyes that are black.
What am I?

A: A giraffe.

Brooke Hopkins (8)
Mendip Green First School, Weston-super-Mare

What Am I?

I have a super loud roar
And I'm as furry as a mouse.
I eat deer and mice.
I'm as tall as a tiger
But I'm not a tiger.
I'm as fast as a cheetah
And as brown as bread.
What am I?

A: A lion.

Stephanie Jowett (8)
Mendip Green First School, Weston-super-Mare

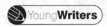

Cats

(Inspired by 'I Think Mice Are Rather Nice' by Rose Fyleman)

I think cats
Are rather silly
Their ears are tall
Their tails are small
They haven't any spots at all
Their legs are pink
Their teeth are white
They race about
The garden at night
They chew things
They shouldn't use
And nobody seems
To like them much
But I think cats are silly.

Eleanor Smith (8)
Mendip Green First School, Weston-super-Mare

The Butterfly

The butterfly is
As pretty as a star.
The butterfly is
As graceful as the wind.
The butterfly is
Lovely, nice and quiet.
The butterfly is beautiful.

Bethany Sim (8)
Mendip Green First School, Weston-super-Mare

Dogs

(Inspired by 'I Think Mice Are Rather Nice' by Rose Fyleman)

I think dogs are rather cute.
Their noses are big,
Their claws are small,
They haven't any hair at all.
Their eyes are white,
Their teeth are white,
They walk about the floor at night.
They lick things,
They shouldn't bite
Because they give you a fright.
Still I think dogs are cute!

Aimee Jones (7)
Mendip Green First School, Weston-super-Mare

Cheetahs - Haikus

Sneaking secretly
Camouflaging in the trees
Prey out there to eat.

I'm in the long grass,
I sneak even closer then
Pouncing on my prey.

I have a big feast
Until someone comes along
Frightened them away

(Just for today!)

Christina Layzell (10)
Preston CE Primary School, Yeovil

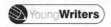

A Dragon Suits Me

People have rabbits,
A fish like a bee,
But the truth is that a dragon,
Will best suit me.

I don't want him to be giant,
Not as small as a rat,
I want him to be tall,
I don't mind if he is fat.

He will fly me to school,
He will take me to Hawaii
But the problem is,
What will I have to buy?

Do I need a big cage?
Do I need five tonnes of meat?
What will he like?
What will he want as a treat?

But do dragons exist?
Will I find one?
And if I find him will he eat me?
Will I become a dead man?

Dionysios Antonopoulos (11)
Preston CE Primary School, Yeovil

Tigers

T is for terrific
I is for integrity
G is for great fun
E is for exciting
R is for tiger's roar
S is for super-duper.

Tony Bailey (11)
Preston CE Primary School, Yeovil

My Best Friend

I have a best friend called Zoe
She is very, very nice
She lives in a house
Which is twice the size of mine.

I have no other friends
She's just the only one
And now it's only me and her
It's heaven in the sun.

Lauren Ann Rice (11)
Preston CE Primary School, Yeovil

My Dog Called Bowe

M y best friend
Y oung at heart

D on't mess with him
O ver the moon with him
G reat at catching a ball.

C learly the best pet in the world
A mazing with all
L ove him to bits
L et him play all day
E very single factor about him is cute
D anced with joy to see him.

B rilliant than a cat
O n the other hand he doesn't let you stop.
W e've had him for ages, he's now nine
E very day it's a delight to see him.

Ellie Hughes (11)
Preston CE Primary School, Yeovil

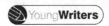

Lewis Turner

My friend is great,
He is my best mate,
We have a good laugh,
He is really fab,
We like to hang out,
We like to shout,
Shout, shout, shout,
We like teasing,
We like meeting,
We ride in the sun,
We have great fun,
We meet on the Xbox,
He beats me 6-1
He is better than me on Black Ops,
But I'm better than him at lots,
He rides a scooter, I ride a bike,
We also like to fly a kite,
We like a fight,
In the light,
I'm better than him,
But he just might,
I like him the best,
He's better than the rest.

Jason McGowan (11)
Preston CE Primary School, Yeovil

Elephant

E ars as big as a giant pothole
L ong flexible trunk to suck up his food
E ndangered species so there's not many
P lants, large footsteps side to side
H as a hilarious face
A hard tough leg
N aughty feet so big it would put you to size
T usks made of ivory.

Rebecca Payne (11)
Preston CE Primary School, Yeovil

My Dad

My sister's dad
Is my dad too
When he gets home
I say, '*I love you!*'

My brother's dad
Is my dad too
When he helps
He's always true.

My dad is fab
He's like my own personal cab
He gets me out of trouble
And pulls me out the rubble.

My dad is great
He is like a big crate of . . .
Happiness!

Teegan Jane Harris (11)
Preston CE Primary School, Yeovil

Dogs!

I have a dog,
She is called Lola,
She loves playing with logs,
And her favourite drink is Cola.

She loves eating leaves,
But she always nicks our keys,
And always pulls on the lead,
And digs out weeds.

She sometimes yelps,
So we try to help,
But she always bites,
And she hates heights.

So this is Lola
She is mad,
But I'm so lucky
And so glad.

Monica Pilkington (11)
Preston CE Primary School, Yeovil

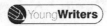

Polar Bear

P olar bears are as white as the snow
O n sunny days they still don't show
L ike a diamond, it's hard to find them
A re they really hard to find?
R eally not many left, it blows my mind.

B ears are vicious but polar bears more
E ating their cubs poor, poor, poor
A nd also very nearly extinct
R eally guys, let's save these lives.

Ollie Page (10)
Preston CE Primary School, Yeovil

Snip-Snap

They walk around side to side,
They jump around with pride
And if you get close,
You will get snapped.

> *Snip-snap!*
> *Snip-snap!*

You will find them on the beach,
Covered in seaweed, the colour of bleach,
They pounce around with delight,
But there's something dangerous in sight.

> *Snip-snap!*
> *Snip-snap!*

Oh no! there's a seagull,
He'll come down and eat you whole!
And make this official the crab has been

> *Snapped!*

Jack Thomas (11)
Preston CE Primary School, Yeovil

Pantomime

Up went the curtain, out stomped an evil man
His skin was a greyish tan,
He had a devious plan

But soon he failed
And began to wail
That was the end of the tale.

The show was good
Next year I should
Go and see it again.

It was funny, men were women, women were men
Then people started laughing again
That was the end, I went round a bend
I got in the car and said, 'Hoorah!'

Adam Strange (9)
St Saviour's CE Junior School, Larkhall

My Mother Saw A Dancing Tiger

My mother saw a dancing tiger
At the train station
With her bonnet and frilly gown
Waiting for the subway
Going to town.

Metal round its neck
Doing a dance
Is it being hurt?
There might be a chance
Stinging its neck,
Falling apart.

Slipping side to side
Doing the glide
Eyes being stunned
Paying a fund
Twisting and turning
Skin was burning.

Emily Mobbs (9)
St Saviour's CE Junior School, Larkhall

Untitled

I'd been pondering all day
And as I stomped out of the car,
I wondered why we
Heard miaowing in the house.

As I unlocked the door
I saw a cat soar
Right past the door
When it saw me and Hattie.

We yelled in surprise
As it raised its head in fright
And one crawled up to my feet.

We called one Dennis
And the other Mia
And nicknamed them both
Den and Miss Mia.

Joel Dale (10)
St Saviour's CE Junior School, Larkhall

The Juggling Man

No coat to cover shoulders bare
When the water turned to ice
Bolder he tried so hard to be
After his stagger, no shelter to come.

Fingers cold and numb balls weaved through
Never feels healthy or happy
Lost in his own nothingness land
Never has notes or pounds in his wallet

Only the yellow tinkling balls
Will make his mind ignore his grief
No family to help him cope
No soothing voice to tell him it's all right.

Ava Piper (9)
St Saviour's CE Junior School, Larkhall

The Emirates Day!

April the 16th
That day was really awesome
To North London I went
By the train.

Saw the Emirates
Sat in the manager's chair
The changing rooms were great
It was brill.

I saw the trophies
In the breathtaking museum
Bought an Arsenal shirt
In their shop.

Matthew Morris (10)
St Saviour's CE Junior School, Larkhall

My Sister's Spectacular Wedding

On the 18th of July
Get prepared for . . .
My sister's spectacular wedding!
Doing our make-up
Early in the morning for . . .
My sister's spectacular wedding!

Trying on our dresses
Doing our fluffy hair for . . .
My sister's spectacular wedding!
Six cute bridesmaids and
Six attractive ushers for . . .
My sister's spectacular wedding!

Walking down the aisle
In our fluttering dresses for . . .
My sister's spectacular wedding!
Kissing the gorgeous groom
He's so handsome in . . .
My sister's spectacular wedding!

Evie Keiller (9)
St Saviour's CE Junior School, Larkhall

The Beach

With the wavy blue waves
Going in and out, in and out.
While the dinghy drivers drift
In and out, in and out of view.

The sandy beaches, the blue sky
Children scoffing ice cream, 'Yum!'
While the waves go out and in
Like kids eating, but sand.

But at the dark dusk it changes
With owls tu-whit tu-whooing all night
The beach, empty, shadowy black
The waves go in and out.

Beach in day, full with kids
But night, starless and deserted
So if you like full, come day
If you like quiet, come night.

Daniel Davey (9)
St Saviour's CE Junior School, Larkhall

Winter Festival

Wonderful winter festival
Marquee on
A muddy rugby field

There were in marquee
Bucking bronco reindeer
Nearby tins full of prizes

Delicious, scrumptious food on sale
Bar open
Drinks, hot dogs, burgers, chilli

Fire jugglers are here
Fake snow on a grotto
Explosions of fireworks.

Cody Richmond (9)
St Saviour's CE Junior School, Larkhall

The Snow

I see people sledging
Children throwing snowballs
Going out to play in the snow
Watching the snow.

Sliding in the car.
Strolling to school on a winter's day.
Feeling the snow.
Walking home from school.

Our car didn't work.
Days off school.
Satisfactory.
Hooray!

Wrapped up nice and warm
Watching the snow fall.
Shivering snow.
Seeing the snow demolish.

Billy Young (10)
St Saviour's CE Junior School, Larkhall

Niagara Falls

The boat pulled up upon the shore.
I heard the engine roar.
Gingerly, I stepped onto the boat and off we soared
Water gleams, it was crystal clear.

Drenched my face, the spray it did.
Trying to escape.
Tumbles over does the water, but yet it never breaks.
Forceful sea, tempest heart.

While upon the promenade.
They dance in morning air.
Sometimes my mind wanders back when we were there.
By Niagara Falls.

Isabel Tanko (9)
St Saviour's CE Junior School, Larkhall

Bath Half Marathon

I joined crowds at the starting line
Adrenalin charged the moist air
Moving, inspiring
Clear blue sky, fresh, sharp.

At the bang of the starting gun
Music blurted out the speakers
Moving, inspiring
Some in fancy dress.

Sprinting so far for charity
Beads of sweat running down their faces
Moving, inspiring -
Bath Half Marathon!

Max Williams-Grey (9)
St Saviour's CE Junior School, Larkhall

Kensington Meadows Festival

The jugglers are juggling from far away,
Whilst the bionic band plays,
From the food, to the fun and firework and sun.

The windy trees, bushes and branches,
Whistling a time of glory,
The fireworks blast into the shine of sun.

A big lot of joy,
From a small little boy,
Dancing to the beat
Stomp his feet
To the sound of the drumbeat.

The unicycle rides,
As the young girl cries
Whilst she is watching McFly.

Darcy Ferris (10)
St Saviour's CE Junior School, Larkhall

Wedding

Wedding, wedding, wedding
In the battlements
Wedding, wedding, wedding
Blessing of the elements.

Wedding, wedding, wedding
On the lawn
Wedding, wedding, wedding
Be cautious of the thorn.

Wedding, wedding, wedding
Bubbles everywhere
Wedding, wedding, wedding
Bubbles around the air.

Wedding, wedding, wedding
Dance to the beat
Wedding, wedding, wedding
This wedding can't be beat.

Zac Woodford (10)
St Saviour's CE Junior School, Larkhall

On The Brecon Beacons

Stunning wild ponies.
Galloping in the morning air,
One was snowy white.
Two were midnight-blue.
Three were chestnut-brown.
Their manes shimmer.
In the illuminated sun.

In the humdrum car.
We talk and talk while time passes.
But then we stop.
At the sight of the gorgeous
Frozen waterfall.

Yasmine Zurian (10)
St Saviour's CE Junior School, Larkhall

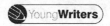

I Went On The London Eye

I went on the London Eye
Way up in the flossy sky.

It was really fun
Looking at the shining sun.

It was high above the river,
It gave me a real shiver.

Moving very smoothly,
Slow and very groovy.

I could see bridges,
Buildings and the face of Big Ben looking at me
A wonderful sight to see.

Afterwards we got some burgers and chips
And lots of yummy dips.

It was time to go home
And I waved goodbye to St Paul's Dome.

I was sad to be on my way
But never mind,
I had an astonishing day!

Suki Acton Peters (10)
St Saviour's CE Junior School, Larkhall

Pitter-Patter, Splish-Splash

It blows in my face, the wind does
Splash in puddles, run for shelter!
I'm getting drenched, run indoors,
Pitter-patter, splish-splash.

Oh no, water is in my eyes!
Splish-splash, water is in my shoes.
Black and heavy, the clouds are too,
Pitter-patter, splish-splash.

It is wet play, hip hip hooray!
On the computer we will play,
Or read a book to make time pass,
Pitter-patter, splish-splash.

The rain slows down, the wind does too,
The sun peeps out behind the clouds.
'Will it clear up?' I ask myself
Pitter-patter, splish-splash.

The sun is shining, brightly now,
Oh yes! Back to the football we go.
Will we finish our game this time?
Shining sun, children on the run.

Bryan Clarke (10)
St Saviour's CE Junior School, Larkhall

One Wedding

I was in a terrific mood
Because there was food,
My mum looked ace,
My dad looked smart,
I was in a tuxedo,
I saw my cousin Georgie,
I ate tomato soup,
My mum wore make-up,
I felt just mild
When my mum and dad kissed,
I had to bring the shiny rings,
I had the meal of my life.

Aimee Grant (9)
St Saviour's CE Junior School, Larkhall

How I Got My Cat

For my birthday of five,
From my mum's friend, a cat.
From a litter of strays,
A tabby and speckled.

Five pussies snuggled to Mum,
But one roaming away.
That one was dotted,
And the rest were all tabby.

Ah! That spotty one's like me!
It has my personality!
I love her! I'd adore her!
That's the one for me!

Oscar Carr-Linford (9)
St Saviour's CE Junior School, Larkhall

A First Pet

On the day of Easter
I awoke
To the smell of pancakes
To the drawing room I go . . .

Three pancakes on a plate
Flavoursome
Kitchen out of bounds!
A strange situation

Finally allowed in
Sky tea towel
Covering a large cube
I pull it away, I gasp!

A large home of metal
Sawdust stuffed
A shining new blue ball,
Marine-blue hamster wheel.

I take a peek inside
Try and hide
I catch a glimpse of you!
You sweet golden brown hamster!

Settle down to pancakes
Always treats
I turn on the telly
Knowing my family is one place bigger.

Olivia Stiles (10)
St Saviour's CE Junior School, Larkhall

Footsteps Agree

We take 1,000 footsteps,
And I'm sure you will agree,
There is no serious attention paid,
To feet, unlike to me!

To achieve life,
And I'm sure you will agree,
That we would be unable,
Without feet, to make the tea!

To leap and dance,
And I'm sure you will agree,
Will be rather exciting
You can do it, at a party!

To meet,
And I'm sure you will agree,
With friends you will need,
Feet, or you will have to pay a fee!

Footsteps support you,
And I'm sure you will agree,
That they have brains,
Footsteps agree, by Josie!

Josie Emmeline Hollin (9)
St Saviour's CE Junior School, Larkhall

Feeling Equine

Two horses in a lush green field,
Only have each other for company,
Grazing gracefully,
Drinking delicately.

A lake at end,
Where horses drink
Clean, fresh, foot deep.

Tufts of grass to graze on,
Sugar cubes to chew on,
A field to run about in,
A paddock to sleep in.

Two horses in a lush green field,
Only have each other for company,
Time to leave,
Close the gate.

Saoirse Fletcher-Read (10)
St Saviour's CE Junior School, Larkhall

Mr Rabbit

M r Rabbit is a sweet little rabbit who travels
R ound the block.

R ound and round the block he goes
A ll with lots of fun
B urrowing deep into his hole all with lots of fun
B ecause he has a family he has to get some food.
I n his hole a little kid and a wife who's lots of fun.
T o his hole with all the food goes Mr Rabbit.

Emily Reed (9)
Salway Ash CE (VA) Primary School, Bridport

This Is Funny

This is funny
I like honey
There's some jam
Ohh, I like ham
I like beans
There's some aubergines
I'm on my knees
Give me some cheese
Start to bake
'Cause I want a cake
Then start slicing
Put on the icing
This is all written on paper
See you later,
Hang on, there's a yeti
Eating my spaghetti!

Nathan Rollett (10)
Salway Ash CE (VA) Primary School, Bridport

Woodland Area

W ishing wells everywhere
O dd humans wander over there
O ld wise crickets sing a song
D oodle flowers give a pong
L ovely ladies water mushrooms
A nd fairy couples kiss in love rooms
N ettle cookies are golden brown
D illy and his friends are making crowns.

A ll the pretty flowers grow
R iffle and his workmen make the horses go
E veryone celebrates round the fire
A ll is quiet apart from the choir.

Eloise Matthews (10)
Salway Ash CE (VA) Primary School, Bridport

Recipe For A Friend

Kind - 250g
Fun - 75g
Humour - 95g
Care - 170g
Trust - 120g
Honesty - 75g
Respect - 85g
Reliability - 160g

Add care with the honesty in a bowl and stir.
It will come out as a yellow, sticky paste.
Add 3 teaspoonfuls of respect to the paste.
While you're stirring you add a bit of humour every now and then.
Reliability will be the last ingredient
Then you put in the kind.

Enjoy the fun!

Jake Rowland (11)
Salway Ash CE (VA) Primary School, Bridport

Silly Sweets

Gobbly gobstoppers
Disgusting liquorice
Chewy Chewits
Bubbly bubblegum
Stupid fizzy pots
Yellow pineapple chunks
Fizzy, fuzzy Vimto
Bouncy boiled eggs
Winny wine gums
Jumping jelly babies
Murky milky buttons
Quality Quality Streets
Perfect Polos
Malty Maltesers.

These are the silly sweets!

Lydia James (9)
Salway Ash CE (VA) Primary School, Bridport

Halloween Night

Ferocious vampires
Zonked zombies
Weird werewolves
Goofy ghosts
The monsters of Halloween Night
Crazy clowns
Bogus bats
Wild witches
Silly spiders
The monsters of Halloween night
Super cyclops
Drab dragons
Awesome ogres
Terrible trolls
The monsters of Halloween night
Anonymous aliens
Murderous monsters
Crazy corpses
Grey gravestones
The monsters of Halloween night
Wiggly wizards
Brushing broomsticks
Terrific tarantulas
Gruesome griffins
The monsters of Halloween night
They will give you a fright.

Samuel Huxter (9)
Salway Ash CE (VA) Primary School, Bridport

Silent Night

The plain is silent.
Suddenly the sky crackles with cosmic power.
A sentinel walks forward as swift as a jaguar.
As silent as a hunter in search of the prey.
It walks after its prey.
In the distance a slight rumble.
Then suddenly a thousand steel monsters move in smashing all in their way
Nought stands in their way.
And monstrous titans of metal and cement have come to play
They are followed by four million thudding feet
They're coming to do what they do best
Run, for they are coming.

Tommy Green (10)
Salway Ash CE (VA) Primary School, Bridport

Mushrooms

Mushrooms are cool.
Mushrooms are colourful.
They have spots all over
And have a brown stalk.
Mushrooms are in Fairyland
Mushrooms love me and I love
Mushrooms!

Georgia Walther (10)
Salway Ash CE (VA) Primary School, Bridport

Time Ticking

T icking away
I n a little rhythm
M aking night and day
E vening and morning too.

T elling me it's dinner time
I rritating sometimes
C hecking it rapidly
K eeping time
I n the car
N othing stops time
G etting ready for bed.

Lexie Jefford (10)
Salway Ash CE (VA) Primary School, Bridport

Witch's Cat

Two yellow, small, bright eyes
Black whiskers sticking out of his face
White, pointed, sharp teeth
Soft, black fur.

James Davidson (11)
Salway Ash CE (VA) Primary School, Bridport

Funky Fish

'I've been working out,' said Mussel.
'I'm priceless,' boasted Goldfish.
'I love Jesus,' cried Angelfish.
'Honk, honk,' squeaked Clownfish.
'Let's shoot some hoops,' shouted Basking Shark.
'Wibble-wobble,' wobbled Jellyfish.
'Hold onto my shoulders,' boogied Conger Eel.
'I'm exhausted,' huffed Pufferfish.
'Please may I have a penny?' begged Sea Urchin.
'Don't eat me,' pleaded Sea Cucumber.
'Night-night,' yawned Starfish.

Joshua William Frampton (9)
Salway Ash CE (VA) Primary School, Bridport

Recipe For A Friend

Ingredients:
1 bed
1 heart
6oz stick up for you
7oz cheerful
4oz funny fun
5oz trust
8oz joyful.

Method:
Put stick up for you in a bowl and stir cheerful with it.
Add the 5oz of trust to the mixture,
Then stir in the 8oz of joyful.
Then pour it in the heart
Then put it in the body
And then put it in the bed.

Will Gibbons (10)
Salway Ash CE (VA) Primary School, Bridport

Randomness

Boats are cool
They sail across the sea
And football is not for me
The colour yellow is very pretty
And I love kitties
Tigers run really fast
As time whizzes past
Dancing is really fun
Can I have an iced bun?
Toadstools are spotty
And ladybugs are polka dotty
You may call me strange
But I'm not going to change!

Jemima Platt (11)
Salway Ash CE (VA) Primary School, Bridport

Darkness

In the darkness my blood goes cold.
In the darkness vampires suck our blood.
In the darkness the witches come.
In the darkness I go to sleep.

Spike Travers (10)
Salway Ash CE (VA) Primary School, Bridport

Teddy Bears

One teddy bear drank some rum.
Two teddy bears went for a run.
Three teddy bears rubbed their tum.
Four teddy bears ate some crossed buns.
Five teddy bears had a chat.
Six teddy bears hid under a mat.
Seven teddy bears played ball and bat!
Eight teddy bears sat.
Nine teddy bears played with a rat.
Ten teddy bears had a nice nap!

Nadia Hadj-Aissa (10)
Salway Ash CE (VA) Primary School, Bridport

Leopard

I want to be a leopard
Sleeping in the sun all day.

I want to be a leopard
Catching my own prey.

I want to be a leopard
Running like the wind.

I am a leopard
In a different way!

Olly Warnes (9)
Salway Ash CE (VA) Primary School, Bridport

Black And Orange Tiger - Haiku

I'm a kind of cat
With black and orange-striped fur
The noise I make - *roar!*

Kirsty Dunford (10)
Salway Ash CE (VA) Primary School, Bridport

The Coming Of Spring

The coming of spring,
Is a beautiful thing,
As plants begin to grow.
The birds are a-chirping.
The seas are a-slurping
And farmers get ready to sow.

Celebrate, celebrate,
Get on and do it before it's too late.
Celebrate, celebrate.
The coming of spring is here.

Snowdrops and daffodils,
Sprout off the hills.
And sheep begin to graze.
The clouds are a-chasing,
The horses are a-racing
And the sun is ablaze.

Celebrate, celebrate,
Get on and do it before it's too late.
Celebrate, celebrate.
The coming of spring is here.

The breeze is all gusty and nothing's left dusty.
As people do a spring clean.
The grass is a-greening.
With sun and with meaning.
Some butterflies are said to be seen.

Natalie Megill (9)
Selwood Anglican/Methodist Middle School, Frome

Snowy Days

Misty like a white gale
Sharp feathers coming to
Attack me whirling around the park
Wind blowing into my face.

Children shouting, screaming
As the snowball comes to get them.
Children going down the hill
Having lots and lots of fun.

Luke Hurrell (9)
Selwood Anglican/Methodist Middle School, Frome

Snowy Poem

Trugging through the misty freezing blanket of tumbling snow
Like an attack of tiny soft white bullets.
People racing down hills, skidding and spinning everywhere.
Out in the fields, people's toes turning to ice cubes.
What am I?
Fluffy,
White,
Snow.

Fin Feeney (10)
Selwood Anglican/Methodist Middle School, Frome

Snow Time

Drifting round the sleepy sky.
Spitting with drips of white.
Snow blankets covering the ground.
The wind whooshed around the town.
Icicle hanging from roof to roof.
People throwing balls of snow.
Lots of children with smiley faces.

Leah Prichard (10)
Selwood Anglican/Methodist Middle School, Frome

Snow Poem

Crunching under my feet.
As I walked to school.
On the pavement
Sticking to my gloves.
The snow melts into my warm hands.

Lydia Ayten Uygaç (9)
Selwood Anglican/Methodist Middle School, Frome

Snow Poem

Drifting round the cold sky
Isolated on the ground like a blanket
Twinkling
Sparkling
Glistening
And blowing like a sandstorm
Fluffy
Crunchy
Misty
Making you feel excited
Because it's snow.

Dominic Kirkwood (10)
Selwood Anglican/Methodist Middle School, Frome

Snowy Day

Winter wonderland
Twinkling in the sunlight
Glistening like crystals
Drifting round the sky in swirls
Looks like feathers from a pillow
Children throwing snowballs so high
Many people making snowmen
Everyone having fun.
Toes going cold
Ears hot red
Hands going numb.

Chloe Hill (9)
Selwood Anglican/Methodist Middle School, Frome

Snow Poem

See-through ice
Squishing footprints that you leave behind
Freezing temperatures from its breeze
Slush on the hard ground
The snow like angels
Snowballs splatter on your face
Icicles dripping from a height.

Jack Williams (10)
Selwood Anglican/Methodist Middle School, Frome

Snow Poem

Like feathers in a pillowcase
Getting in your hair
It's a misty feeling
Freezing the countryside
Glistening in the air
Snow whirling everywhere
It's a magical sound
Crunching on the ground.

Adam Warwick (10)
Selwood Anglican/Methodist Middle School, Frome

What Am I?

A soft blanket of a white, crunchy carpet,
Tiny feathers, twinkling merrily,
Sparkling fairy dust appears magically,
What am I?
I am . . .
Fluffy,
White,
Snow!

Holly Davis (9)
Selwood Anglican/Methodist Middle School, Frome

World War I

As the winter winds,
Swoop over the hill,
The rattling of planes
Are strongly heard.

The trenches lay under,
The open ground
Covered with mud and dirt,
With the men crouching by the side.

The gunshot fires,
The men stand up straight,
And still once more,
With a rifle at their side.

All over the country people
Worry about their loved ones,
While the soldiers fight for peace
And let their loyalty show.

Men fought to protect their country
So every man and every woman
Should stand proud for what their country has achieved.

Charlotte Baker (10)
Selwood Anglican/Methodist Middle School, Frome

Snowy Days

S now is very cold
N ips your nose
O ver fields and houses
W hite, feathery flakes, floating down
Y oung children playing in the snow.

D angerous driveways
A ll cars hidden
Y et to be found
S now falls from the sky.

Megan Bee-Pringle (10)
Selwood Anglican/Methodist Middle School, Frome

Hope

Hope is what gets you out of bed in the morning.
It's what makes you try in a test,
When you have not revised.
Hope will never tell you that you can't,
Because hope knows that you can do anything.
Hope is that glimmer of light at the end of a dark tunnel.
Hope is like God, it loves, and supports everybody.
It made apes evolve into Man,
It made me write this poem,
I want this poem to win,
Hope needs this read out,
Because it knows that this can change people.
When you fail two times,
Hope will make you try a third.

Daniel Plausin (11)
Selwood Anglican/Methodist Middle School, Frome

Snowy Days

Drifting round the sleepy sky
Covering the ground like a white shower
Crunching under my feet
Falling to the ground like small isolated feathers
All hail winter.

Icicles hanging from roof to roof
Quiet as a stalker
What am I . . . ?
Fluffy,
White,
Cold,
Snow! Snow! Snow!

Melissa Cook (10)
Selwood Anglican/Methodist Middle School, Frome

Snowy Days

Glistening, shimmering in the sunlight,
Feathers falling out of the clouds
Drifting round the sleepy sky,
A frozen carpet on the ground.

Children screeching, 'Oi!' at their dads.
Getting cold before you move.
Going, *Brrr!* every second.
Before you know it your dad is running away.

Frozen nose and toes,
Your ears are fit to burst with coldness.

A never-ending adventure just waiting to happen,
The snow is on its way.

Cameron Gazard (9)
Selwood Anglican/Methodist Middle School, Frome

How To Make A Rainbow

Rainbow, rainbow way up high
Filled with colours in the sky.
If the weather is quite cold
The things that turn to ice are the things that you hold.
And at the end of the day
When the clouds have gone away.
The sun comes out
Then a rainbow starts to sprout.
The rainbow then glimmers
Then it starts to shimmer.
It fills the whole neighbourhood
With bright colours and you know it would.

Rosie Le Lohé Attwell (9)
Selwood Anglican/Methodist Middle School, Frome

Winter Poem

Spinning around
Until it gently lands on the ground
Children throwing snowballs at someone's door.

Feels like an elephant squirting my feet,
I get icicles hanging from my nose.

Looks like a tornado
Going through the town,
Blowing people's gloves way up high.

Adam Kerslake (10)
Selwood Anglican/Methodist Middle School, Frome

Winter Poem

Twirling snow blowing everywhere
Floating in the sky
Children throwing snowballs
High into the air
A giant's blowing at your feet
A blanket falling on the world
Lots of pieces of paper ripped apart
Like a white tornado.

James Hancock (10)
Selwood Anglican/Methodist Middle School, Frome

Snow Poem

Glistening in the sunlight
Twinkling in the moonlight
Feathers whooshing down
From the deep blue sky
Going this way then that way
Swirling about
Then landing on the freezing ground, like magic.
All making a winter wonderland, with snow.

Connor Cairns (10)
Selwood Anglican/Methodist Middle School, Frome

Snow Poem

Twirling round and round
In the bitter cold wind,
Floating like feathers,
Settling as it makes a blanket.
Drifting round the sleepy sky,
Crunching under my feet as I walk to school.
Looks like the clouds have fallen far down from Heaven above,
As fluffy as a teddy bear.
The trees turn white overnight whilst it snows.
The streets start to glimmer
As the sun comes out,
Making footprints when people stomp by,
Spreading in the countryside
Like a field of cotton wool.

Lauren Mead (10)
Selwood Anglican/Methodist Middle School, Frome

Snowy Day

Winter wonderland
Twinkling and twirling
Fluffy little piles
Icicles dangling.

Shimmering snowmen
Slithering sledges
Shining snowballs
Falling fairies.

Warm coat
Fuzzy feeling
White wellies
Freezing feet.
Wild bright sky.

Tilly Lunt (9)
Selwood Anglican/Methodist Middle School, Frome

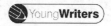

Spring Poem

Fantastic flowers, beautifully blossoming.
Kind kids, quietly gossiping.
Amazing animals coming out of hibernation.
We live in a fantastic nation.
Colourful birds singing sweet songs.
Hopefully it will last long.
The lovely, hot, bright sun.
I love kisses from my mum.
So at last it's here.
Let it be a good year.
Let's have a nice spring
So come and sing!

Chloe Eacott (10)
Selwood Anglican/Methodist Middle School, Frome

The Beach

Standing in the shallow sea
Salty water to my knee
Sand stuck in-between your toes
Slap on lots of suncream so not to burn your nose.

Ice cream dripping down my face
Chocolate vanilla in the wrong pace
Melting, melting on my plate
Crabs come along and eat my lace.

Standing in the shallow sea
Time to go home for my tea
My soggy feet and I
Have a bath and say goodbye.

Eleanor Robilliard (11)
Stoberry Park School, Wells

Planes

A giant metal bird some people say,
A furious 1,050 miles per hour
Gliding to many different countries,
'Oh wow! Oh wow! I am very tired,
Replied the plane up in the air.

A plane, a plane, number 136,
Is very tired and very long
Up in the air it swoops down from the sky.

A plane, a plane, number 136,
Glides gracefully through the air,
'Hello, are you there Captain Carl?'
On plane 136 there is a storm coming quick.

A plane, a plane, number 136,
Plane 136, please steady on girl,
'Let's take our chance and take the landing!'

Emily Owen (10)
Stoberry Park School, Wells

In My Mind There Is . . .

Some dust of IO,
The beak of a flying flower,
A corner of a triangle,
And half of an ostrich's wing.

In my mind there is . . .

A tear of a weeping fly,
The first ever song of a whale,
A view from the Hubble telescope,
And the tip of a jousting pike.

In my mind there is . . .

A thousand years of wear and tear,
The glittering stars of the galaxy x 9,
The thigh bone of a hyena
And a snake from the head of Medusa.

Harry Stein (11)
Stoberry Park School, Wells

Chips!

Chips come in all sizes,
Chunky, oven, mini, French fries.
I know we all love them,
But there are a lot of lies.

Once you buy them from the shop,
Now you'll get a massive shock,
The best bit is the spine,
But everyone calls, 'That's mine!'

Just to put you through this pain,
The fluffy bit is your brain,
This next bit will kill your nose,
The crispy outside is your toes!

Sorry that we had to tell,
Have you let out a horrible yell?
But anyway it would reveal
That now you will not have that meal.

So next time you want a chip,
Make sure you kiss it on the lip!

Izzy Mills-Smith (9)
Stoberry Park School, Wells

My Talking Marshmallow

Jumps and bumps
Round the kitchen table
Up and down, all around
Whilst singing to my friends
My talking marshmallow
Is pink and fluffy
Very, very small
But I love my talking marshmallow
He is the best of all.

Charlie Nicholls (11)
Stoberry Park School, Wells

My Three Dogs

My dog Kenny,
Lying in his bed.
My dog Kenny,
Has a big head.

My dog Theo,
Jumps on chairs.
My dog Theo,
Chewed his teddy bear.

My dog Bovril,
Likes to bite.
My dog Bovril,
Has a kite.

My dog Kenny,
Faster than fast.
My dog Kenny,
Wears a cast.

My dog Theo,
Barks at cars.
My dog Theo,
Jumps over bars.

My dog Bovril,
Likes to fight.
My dog Bovril,
Breaks big lights.

My three dogs,
Keep me entertained.
My three dogs,
Love me again.

Ed Purchase (10)
Stoberry Park School, Wells

A Tiger

Raw meat eater.
Razor teeth.
Brilliant eyesight.
Ginger black.
Stripy slinker.
Dark prowler.
A fast runner.
Strikes like a snake.
Bites like an anaconda.
Two layers of striking teeth.

Dylan Kenniston-Powell (9)
Stoberry Park School, Wells

Ivy

The ivy
Wriggling up the wall
Long, beautiful and tall
Like a snake on the wall
And like an elastic band
With green jelly babies hanging off
Ivy is beautiful
It makes me feel small.

Ella Garrett (11)
Stoberry Park School, Wells

Snakes

Beady bright beastly eyes,
Their silky, slimy, slithery skin
Gliding through the grass,
Razor-red fangs dripping with thick blood;
Sensational, sensitive smell hunting down their prey!
Their mega murderous mouths swallowing dinner whole!
Lethal vicious venom squirting silently at its meal,
Death dealing danger through the park!
Mortal humans
Beware!

Imogen Stocker (9)
Stoberry Park School, Wells

My Special Place

In my special place
I can be who I want
I can live how I want
I can do what I want

In my special place
I can hear what I want
The rush of a river
The swish of a cape
The creaky door of a haunted house

In my special place
I can touch what I want
The cheek of a baby
The feather of a hummingbird
A shooting star

In my special place
I can smell what I want
A fresh baked cake
A bale of hay
The fear of an old man's dying day
That's my special place, what's yours?

Maya Blackwell (11)
Stoberry Park School, Wells

Dingo

Bounding, bouncing along.
Some dingoes making a pong.
Having a wonderful time.
Never missing a chime.
Suddenly they pounce
At a bypassing mouse.
Pointy, pricked-up ears.
Never sheds their tears.

Oscar Harethwaites (10)
Stoberry Park School, Wells

I Wish I Did Not Have To Go To Sleep

I wish I did not have to go to sleep
It's a waste of my time.
It's boring, bad and annoying.
I don't like it at all.

I wish I did not have to go to sleep
There's so much more to do, like playing on my Xbox
Or running around outside.
I wish I did not have to go to sleep
When I could be doing things outside
Having so much fun.
I wish I did not have to go to sleep.
I wish I could be doing something else
Other than sleeping.

Matthew Wood (10)
Stoberry Park School, Wells

Vampire

Vampire
Cold, vicious,
Venomous bite
Vampire
Coffin sleeper
Red eyes
Vampire
Slow walker
Bloodsucker
Vampire
Pale skin
Black wearer
Vampire
You would never
Want to meet one.

Ellen Messenger (11)
Stoberry Park School, Wells

My Dog

My dog,
His name is Sam
And Sam likes ham.
In the morning he jumps up
But he's such a clever pup.
My dog,
He knows loads of tricks
But it really hurts when he kicks.
We make him sit for his tea
And he goes in the garden to have a wee.
My dog,
I love him so very much
And he used to live in a hutch!
My brother calls him Sammy boy
And Monkey is his favourite toy!

Phoebe Dimambro (9)
Stoberry Park School, Wells

A Cat

Fluffy and fat,
Smooth, furry, lively,
As sleepy as a bat,
Like a rabbit in a hat,
It makes me feel like a giant,
Like a beast up in the sky,
A cat
Reminds us that we have to look after our pets.

Ellen Kinder (10)
Stoberry Park School, Wells

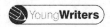

A Beautiful Bunny

Lives in a hutch
Fluffy, small, lively
As cute as a kitten
Like a hopping kangaroo
It makes me feel giant
Like a beast in the woods
A bunny
Reminds me to look after animals.

Hannah Walker (10)
Stoberry Park School, Wells

A Lollipop

Edible and on a stick.
Filling, yummy, sticky,
As if you can't stop eating them.
Like they're the best sweet ever!
It makes me feel giddy, like a bumpy car journey.
A lollipop,
It reminds me how popular they can be.

Isabelle Harris (10)
Stoberry Park School, Wells

A Kitten

Very cute
Fluffy, small and joyful
As fast as a cheetah
As playful as a puppy
It makes me feel as happy
As a child at a party.
As ginger as some marmalade
As cute as a bunny
Reminds me of my cats.

Harriet Chinn (9)
Stoberry Park School, Wells

A Delicate Dewdrop

A delicate dewdrop,
On a delicate web,
A delicate web on a tree branch,
A delicate tree in a vast forest,
A delicate vast forest on a planet,
A delicate planet in a solar system,
A delicate solar system of vast wetland,
A delicate vast Milky Way in deep space,
A delicate dewdrop in deep space,
A delicate dewdrop in space,
All part of the human race.

Benjamin Carver (10)
Stoberry Park School, Wells

Hot Chocolate

Warm and nice
Like cuddly mice
As the clock strikes twice
The hot steam is nice.

Brendan Patrick Jones (11)
Stoberry Park School, Wells

Spider

Has eight legs
Very hairy
Sneaky thing
Creepy as well
Black as the night
Scary face
Horrible body
Clings on to its web.

Susie Brooke (9)
Stoberry Park School, Wells

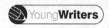

The Killer Rabbits

Every time I go outside, they're always by the door,
They're smelly, fast and ugly-looking,
All I want to do is go to the park,
Rabbits, rabbits, rabbits, who would want to have rabbits?
They're only scared of cats and bats, they're scared of nothing else,
Maybe I better get a cat or a bat.
My mum is most likely not going to give me another pet,
I just hate looking into those eyes,
So red-looking,
They're always chasing me,
Especially biting me,
I've still got that scar on my face,
They're always weeing on me,
Their claws are so long,
I never can go to the park with my friends,
I hate my rabbits,
Only if I had a cat or a bat,
Life would be so much better.

Daniel Newman (11)
Stoberry Park School, Wells

A Kitten

Tiny and quiet
Fluffy, cuddly, fast
As cute as a fluffy puppy
As feisty as a lion
As beautiful as a model
I feel like I'm cuddling a furball
I'm as happy as someone going to Florida
A kitten
It always brings me happiness.

Hannah Tidball (10)
Stoberry Park School, Wells

The Phoenix Bird

Fire bird that blazes the night,
Your wings like gold,
As you take flight,
Red as flames your tail feathers gleam,
When you nest,
Slow and steady you seem,
Your talons are sharp, your beak is fine,
Your eyes so cold,
But yet they shine,
Wind or rain you fly so far,
Like a blazing comet,
Or a shooting star,
Grey and old you grow each day,
Your final words,
That you must say,
'I'll burn so quick, just like a flash,
But soon I shall
Be reborn from ash.'
Life is earned but death will follow
And then the world
Shall fill with sorrow!

Tom Purchase (11)
Stoberry Park School, Wells

Chinchilla

Super fast
Fluffy, cute, small
Like a fluffy ball of wool
Fast as a cheetah
Makes me glow inside
Like the sun on a hot day
I'd give anything for him.

Oliver Selby (9)
Stoberry Park School, Wells

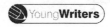

Love Canary

He's lived up to eight years
Little, energetic, fast
As minuscule as two shrews
A beak as sharp as an arrow
He is cute as possible
He reminds me of a feathered pillow.

Ben Swift (10)
Stoberry Park School, Wells

Bear

Fragile fur
Smelly smell
Terrifying teeth
Clashing claws
Sniffing nose
Beast of the woods.

Stacey McKeegan (11)
Stoberry Park School, Wells

A Friend

A friend
Sensible person
Kind, helpful and sweet
Sweet as a strawberry
Playful as a puppy
Fast as a rocket
A friend
I am glad I have a good friend.

Cheyenne Rowlinson-Coombs (10)
Stoberry Park School, Wells

The Crystal

Glittering in the sunlight
I watch it with glee,
Just it sitting there
Looks amazing to me.

Glittering in the sunlight
Sits a lovely quartz,
Gold as the eyes
Of twelve hungry hawks.

Glittering in the sunlight
Clear as a windowpane,
You could even see it
Half a mile down the lane.

Glittering in the sunlight
Resting on a ledge,
It's so bright you can see
It through the hedge.

Glittering in the sunlight
Just gone past three days,
Looks like it's glowing
In the sun's warming rays.

Glittering in the sunlight
Sitting in my chair,
I notice two quartz
Standing in a pair.

Glittering in the sunlight
The beautiful rocks shine,
But you can't have any . . .
Afraid they're all mine.

Charlie Owen Price (11)
Stoberry Park School, Wells

Christmas

Christmas Eve
A night to behold
'Go to bed early'
We get told
'Or presents decrease, tenfold!'

Santa brings games and toys
To girls and boys
But only if they're fast asleep
And do not creep
Around at night
Waiting to see the sight.

Christmas Day brings fun and joy
With children getting many a toy
But do remember girls and boys
Do not creep
On Christmas Eve
When you should be
Fast asleep
Ssshhh!

Harvey John Williams (11)
Stoberry Park School, Wells

A Brain

Lives in your head,
Slimy, brainy and yuck
Like all your guts,
As slimy as a frog,
Makes me more clever,
A brain,
Reminds me of worms
And use it.

Lauren Wakley (11)
Stoberry Park School, Wells

A Dog

Very fluffy
Fast, cute, bit vicious (depends)
Like a bolt of lightning
It makes me want to squeeze it
Like a baby cuddling a teddy.
A dog
Reminds me how long our life is.

Carlos Pople (10)
Stoberry Park School, Wells

Rugby Is The Nation's Game

Dangerous, scary and funny
It's as noisy as WWII.
As rough as cage fighting
My first love
As excited as a champion
Rugby is the nation's game.

Ishi Eyo Nissi Kane (9)
Stoberry Park School, Wells

Football Rules The World

It's a world game
Crunching tackles
Screaming crowds
Sudden death goals
And dramatic

Silky skilled dribbling
In the torrential rain
Pouring down like hailstones
He shoots, he scores!

Jack Madden (9)
Stoberry Park School, Wells

By The Sea

Alone by the sea,
You and me.
We skip along the edge,
Splashing by the window ledge.

Alone by the sea,
You and me.
We spend all day together,
No matter what the weather.

Alone by the sea,
You and me.
Let's just relax,
And watch the drip,
Of the candle wax.

Alone by the sea,
You and me.
Scuffing up the sand,
Walking hand in hand.

Erin Collins (11)
Stoberry Park School, Wells

Tree

There since WWI.
It is gigantic, long, massive.
The tree is like a building.
I am happy, excited.
I am happy like a monkey.
There since WWI.

Chris Thompson (10)
Stoberry Park School, Wells

My Paintbrush

With a swish of my paintbrush,
I can show my feelings
My thoughts, myself,
My personal peelings.

I can make a world,
For no one but me,
A personal place,
Where you need a key.

I'm all alone
In this little place,
There's no one here,
Except my pale face.

It all comes from my paintbrush!

Julia McGiveron (11)
Stoberry Park School, Wells

A Dragon

With broad wings on shoulders,
And a tail of armour,
It stares at me, confused,
I could have sworn it wasn't in my rucksack before.

With eyes of emerald,
And claws like curved daggers,
It seems it's frozen time,
Is this a dream, it can't be?
It's too realistic.

Beating its wings, it flies off into the deep
Maze of the sky.

Rachel Lee (10)
Stoberry Park School, Wells

My Pet Elephant

My pet elephant,
Is called Fred,
His best friend,
Is called Ted.

My pet elephant,
Likes to dance,
Ted the teddy,
Likes to prance.

My pet elephant,
Is as round as a melon,
His favourite food,
Is a sour lemon.

My pet elephant,
He likes to draw,
But he's very naughty,
It's on the floor.

My pet elephant,
Is so great.
I love him more,
Every day.

Karli Rowlinson-Coombs (11)
Stoberry Park School, Wells

My House

My house,
Built in Victorian times,
Grand, spectacular, stony.
As old as the Earth.
As big as the moon,
It makes me feel safe.
Like a palace made of pillows,
My house,
Reminds me of comfort.

Jamie Armstrong-Hughes (9)
Stoberry Park School, Wells

The Mystery Of The Car's Technology

Beneath the bonnet lurks the engine
Put the key in the ignition and turn
A loud roaring sound begins
A cloud of smoke comes out of the exhaust
Wheels begin to turn
Wheels spinning round and round like a washing machine
Spark plugs winking at the petrol.

A fan to keep you cold on a hot day
Liquids washing down through the pipes
Sun reflecting off the wing mirrors
Lighting up the whole car like a torch
Pull up the handbrake
We've reached the end.

Jamie Harris (9)
Stoberry Park School, Wells

I Will Put In My Pocket

(Based on 'Magic Box' by Kit Wright)

I will put in my pocket . . .
A great white shark fin,
The fur of a kitten and also a mitten,
A gentle wave of the massive ocean.

I will put in my pocket . . .
A roaring great lion,
The tusk of a gigantic mammoth
And also my silky blanket
And the antlers of a deer.

I will put in my pocket . . .
The glittering galaxy,
An oink of a pig
And the tail of a fluffy bunny.

Parris Parsons (10)
Stoberry Park School, Wells

School

Why do I have to go to school,
I really do not know,
I could be doing other things
Like eating loads of food.
Pizza, pies and pink prawns.
Pizza is tasty as an ice cream.

School, school boring as a room with nothing in it.
School is like roughing up my road.
How bad is school, bad, bad, bad.
I learnt a lot now
I should go to work.
I cannot be bothered to do maths, literacy and RE.
The best subject is PE and art.

Ethan Kennedy Jennings (10)
Stoberry Park School, Wells

Super Car

Your top speed, 50mph
Fast, cool and loud
And as uncommon as a needle in a haystack.
Your onboard computer is as intelligent as a super computer
And it makes me feel perfect
With chips as my meal.

I can't wait to watch football out the window.
Because all my TVs had broke.
Super car you're very precious to me
Because you show everyone how cool I am.
Oh super car
You make me feel happy when I'm sad
Even when it's raining.

Steven Kockaya (11)
Stoberry Park School, Wells

My Heart

(Based on 'Magic Box' by Kit Wright)

I will put in my heart . . .
The love of the world
And spirit in life.
Happiness and tranquillity.

I will put in my heart . . .
Everyone I love,
And God.

I will put in my heart . . .
The whole world.

I will put in my heart . . .
You and me . . .

Lucy Blight-Mason (11)
Stoberry Park School, Wells

My Box

(Based on 'Magic Box' by Kit Wright)

I will put in my box . . .
A peacock's feather.

I will put in my box . . .
Love hearts for me and you.

I will put in my box . . .
A peacock's feather,
They tickle me right under my chin.

I will put in my box . . .
A big soft pillow
For my little yellow chick
To snuggle up on.

Charlotte Aldridge (10)
Stoberry Park School, Wells

The River

The river sparkles in the sun.
It's always running round and round.
Up and down the river flows.
It's like a star in the sky.
Its amazing sparkles catch my eye.

Katy Nutley (9)
Stoberry Park School, Wells

Valentine Delight

As I was baking I thought,
The cupcake stand I bought,
For my sweetie would be exciting.
I'll make the cakes with sparkly icing.

He'd sent me a dozen of the reddest roses,
The perfume delightful to our noses,
Chocolates in a heart-shaped box,
And a pair of woolly, spotty socks.

We'll dine in for two with M&S,
A brilliant meal that costs us less,
Vanilla candles by the fire,
While we listen to a romantic choir.

Gabriella Tolley (11)
Stoberry Park School, Wells

In My Box . . .

In my box there is something special.
No one is allowed in it.
I always hide it in my bedroom every day.
It is so fragile that it will break.
It's in the shape of an oval
And I like it.
It comes in all different colours
My one is blue with little black dots
And if you haven't noticed
It's an egg in a golden box.

Morgan Parsons (11)
Stoberry Park School, Wells

I Will Put In My Car

(Based on 'Magic Box' by Kit Wright)

I will put in my car . . .
A nice soft blanket
I won't fall asleep on the car seat
I won't fall asleep as I'm going to the beach.

I will put in my car . . .
My soft Labrador
Don't eat all the sandwiches cos you will be given more
You'll be fat, you'll be skinny
You'll be really, really skinny.

I will put in my car . . .
A cuddly toy for my dog to go to sleep
As I'm trying to drive
Stop clambering all over me
Go to sleep doggy, for me.

I will put in my car . . .
A big box of hearts bursting out
This I will put in my car.

Emily Williams (10)
Stoberry Park School, Wells

My Brain

(In the style of Michael Rosen)

My brain
It whirrs around
It's pink, it's in my head, it thinks!
Oooh! A bright pink car.

My brain
It whirrs around
It's pink, in my head it thinks!
Yum-yum strawberry jam.

My brain
It whirrs around
It's pink, it's in my head, it thinks!
Ah-ah! The man on the moon.

Amy Edwards (9)
Stoberry Park School, Wells

I Will Put In My Safe

(Based on 'Magic Box' by Kit Wright)

I will put in my safe . . .
The tusk from an elephant
The salt from the sea
The shell from a turtle
The bark from a tree
The bubbles a fish blows
The ink from a pen
The miaow of a cat
And the feathers from a bird.

Shaquille Coon (11)
Stoberry Park School, Wells

The Painting Of Doom

(In the style of Michael Rosen)

I was looking at a painting one day
Until I heard a scream
I ran quickly into a room
That was filled with steam.

The painting on the wall
Had gobbled up the gentleman
Then spat out all the naughty bits
Which landed in a pan.

I stood at the door
With extreme astonishment
As the painting started speaking words
I wondered what it meant.

Morgan Elms (10)
Stoberry Park School, Wells

My Box

(Based on 'Magic Box' by Kit Wright)

I will put in my box . . .
A soft silk blanket to keep me warm.
A pile of books to read every day.

I will put in my box . . .
A pile of sand to feel through my soft fingers.
The sea as thick as the wind.

I will put in my box . . .
A pack of pencils.
A bright colour of paints.
I'm happy every day.

Elishia Evans (9)
Stoberry Park School, Wells

Love Charlie

(In the style of Roald Dahl)

I love your tabby fur
I love the way you purr
I love the way you eat
I think you're so neat
When your ears prick up
You know I love you
When your tail goes down
The world goes round.

If in the night there's a crash or bang,
In the house I know it's you catching a mouse,
Through the pans, cans and pots
And china cups with spots
You will get him no matter what.
You will be there after school
And before, waiting by the door.

Rose Abbott (11)
Stoberry Park School, Wells

Cinderella

(In the style of Roald Dahl)

Cinderella was ready for the ball,
But then she realised she wore nothing at all,
Then the fairy godmother appeared and said,
'The clothes you want are on your bed.'

Cinderella stood still in shock,
As on her bed was an ugly smock,
She gasped in horror, 'That won't do!
I was after a dress that is brand new!'

With a wave of a wand, the dress transformed,
And on the table it performed,
A little jig for an hour,
Showing off its special power.

'Wow!' shouted Cinderella,
'I'm sure I'll meet my special fella.'
She grabbed the dress and put it on,
Tying up the red ribbon.

The ball she said was so much fun,
But her stepsister wasn't done.
She swapped the shoe with one of her own,
Next week she took the royal throne.

Hannah Robinson (10)
Stoberry Park School, Wells

Horrible Chocolate Cake

(In the style of Roald Dahl)

Chocolate cake, chocolate cake
That's what I don't want when I awake
Melting in your mouth
Especially when you're in the south.

Every little crumb
Makes my stomach go numb
On a delicious chart
There's no point in chocolate cake taking part.

Sticky pudding makes me complete
It's my favourite treat
I love having a dream
About ice cream.

I'd rather throw chocolate cake away
Then eat it another day.
'Cause I'm feeling very ill
I'm gonna go take some pills.

Caleb Ford (11)
Stoberry Park School, Wells

The Mountains

Wailing wind blows over the mountains
A racing river crashes against the rocks
The shining sun glows over the mountains
And melted ice cream drips slowly
Candyfloss clouds stand over the mountains
Freezing ice cracks and melts
Hard chocoate blocks stand by the river
And beautiful birds glide over the ice.

Rosie Mallory (10)
The Epiphany School, Bournemouth

The Dance Of The Rainforest

Deep in the jungle where all the vines grow,
Lays a forest that no one should know.
The pythons slither and the frogs start to hop,
As the rainforest starts the treetop bop.

Plants start to grow and monkeys hum,
Waiting for the rain to come,
Yet sure enough, the rain starts to fall,
Pounding the trees, which then grow tall.

Vines feel the rhythm and jaguars howl,
Gibbons squeal and the forest starts to growl,
The darkness knows that the time is near,
When the animals start to disappear.

And sure enough, without a trace,
The forest stops its little race,
The presence fades and then goes with a *pop!*
Because it knows that it's time to stop.

Alex Wisdom (11)
The Epiphany School, Bournemouth

Our Planet

The sea is like running athletes heading for gold,
The clouds are like fluffy sheep, cuddly and old.
The trees are giant people reaching for the stars,
The moon is shining brightly down, watching from afar.
The parrots in the jungle squawk all night and day,
The camels in the desert know how to find their way.
The mountains stand like giants all covered in snow,
The volcanoes give violent rumbles from the core below.
The sky is ever changing from blue, to black, to grey,
The sun is coming up bringing warmth and light on its way.
The thunder clashes loudly then lightning has its say,
The rain will follow shortly bringing fog and snow today.
Our planet is amazing, there is so much to see,
There is nowhere in the universe that I would rather be.

Cherrie Jones (11)
The Epiphany School, Bournemouth

Spring

S unny early mornings
P eople watching new life arise
R ain still visiting us
I cy mornings
N ights still getting dark early
G od created our beautiful world.

Spring!

Courtney Watts (10)
The Epiphany School, Bournemouth

Flamingo

F orgive
L ife
A nd
M e
I 'll
N ever
G o
O n.

Sophie-Louise Hughes (10)
The Epiphany School, Bournemouth

School Daydream

My alarm went off and had woken me
It was Tuesday morning, it was school again
I wish it could have been a Sunday
We could be laying on the beach or playing in the bay
But it was all a dream
School is not too far away
Really we're in break time, so I will play, play, play!

Casey Rouillier (7)
The Epiphany School, Bournemouth

The Himalayas

The mountain howls as the snow steadily builds in size,
Hurtling down the mountain.
It listens carefully as the snow crashes into the small river,
Sending spray to dampen the mountain's chilly feet.
The mountain shines blindingly as the sun reflects its brilliant gaze on the snow below,
And awakens fully for the blissful day ahead.
A skier speeds down the belly of the mountain,
Disturbing it from its peaceful sleep.

The snow starts to fall lazily,
Drifting where the wind takes it.
Layer upon layer of beautiful snow,
The mountain sags under the weight.
The fir trees shake off the dazzling white blanket from their evergreen leaves,
As the sun relaxes and brightens its gaze.
The buzz of the ski-lifts gently lull the mountain to sleep,
Drifting off into a wonderful fantasy world.

As all is calm,
The sun vanishes behind the sleeping mountain.
A snow leopard is out on a midnight prowl,
Energy replenished and in for the kill.
A young deer hops energetically back to its grazing grounds,
Totally unaware of the danger.
A roar breaks the silence instantly,
But the mountain is not awoken . . .

Isabelle Gillett (11)
The Epiphany School, Bournemouth

A Beach Disaster

I was sitting on the beach one day
A beautiful summer's day in May
Just as I was about to play
A mangle-faced pirate said I had to pay
So I quickly got up and ran away

As I sprinted from that place
Some boys thought I was having a race
So they decided to play chase
Then I fell flat on my face

I saw a flask with an extraordinary task
It said I had to wear a strange mask
I wondered why, so I went to ask
A man at the shop said to find the treasure
All you need to do is measure.

When I got home Gran said, 'Come here,
Are you okay my dear?'
'Yes,' I lied.
'Don't be stupid! You nearly died!'

Sophie Hu (9)
The Epiphany School, Bournemouth

Sunny Seaside

Water rushing from the sea,
Sand blowing in my face,
Children playing, having fun,
And adults relaxing in the sun!
Ice cream, ice cream, blueberry, vanilla,
They're all so tasty,
With sprinkles too,
I hope there's enough for my friend, Lou!
I love the seaside, it's sunny and great,
I want to come back, before it's too late!

Daniella Mallory (10)
The Epiphany School, Bournemouth

The Finest Dish

The wicked witch peered in her cauldron,
To see lots of stinky children
She added salt, pepper and spices,
And just a few apple slices,
She gave a stir; one, two, three
And added carefully a large queen bee.

This would be her finest dish,
Of which her jealous sisters could only wish,
Bubbling, spitting, splashing broth,
That clearly would make her sisters cough,
Nearly ready, couldn't wait any longer,
The grumbling tummies were getting stronger.

Meanwhile outside a woodcutter was lingering about,
His mind made up without a doubt
He swung his axe with all his might,
And soon the witch was out of sight.

Jessie Calvert (9)
The Epiphany School, Bournemouth

Flowers

I like flowers, they're pretty to me,
I count them all; one, two, three,
If I was a flower, a big red rose,
My owner would water me with a hose,
There's only one problem, if I die,
I won't get to see what winter is like,
I would live in the ground as happy as can be,
And see the world from under a tree.
It would be fun being a flower,
I can tell you that,
And I would recommend it, that's a fact.

Erin Padley (9)
The Epiphany School, Bournemouth

It's Bath Time!

When I'm in the bath,
I like to laugh,
I crash, bash and splash,
With my rubber ducky dash!
I like to run and play,
But my tray is in the way.
The bay at the sea,
Is like a bumblebee!

Ellanor Finlayson (9)
The Epiphany School, Bournemouth

Now Here's A Young Puppy

Now here's a young puppy
Who's just so sweet
With her small white tail
And oversized feet;

With her long red tongue
And eyes deeply brown
Her tail always wagging
A patch on her crown

But she's full of trouble
Which can sometimes be fun
As these tales have told me
That the fun has just begun.

One day you'll discover
What all puppies do
They're nice and they're naughty . . .
They sound just like you!

Lauren Gird (10)
The Epiphany School, Bournemouth

Resistance In The Getting Up Period

'Oh c'mon! Time to get up!' I exclaimed to myself.
'But this bed is so comfortable and warm.' I retorted.
'No, no, no! You have work this morning!' I yelled to myself.
'You must get up now otherwise you won't get that promotion you wanted!'
'Of course! Of course!'
I answered myself in a panicked way. Who was I convincing?
'Come in here, have a wash, freshen up,' called the shower.
I reluctantly stormed into the bathroom.
I turned on the tap and felt the soothing hot water on my back.
'Thank you for your service.'
I then put my clothes on but my socks
Seemed to be hiding away from me.
I headed downstairs and then I put the bread in the toaster.
But the bread kept bouncing out again.
'Stop trying to toast me!'
So I went to work without any breakfast.
But I did get the promotion I wanted!

William Hammerton (10)
Wellington Junior School, Wellington

In The Morning

My alarm clock shrieks and yells
I wake.
I sit up and fall out of bed.
My bed implores, 'Don't go!'
I put on my socks and clothes.
My old clothes head for the laundry.
They resist, 'Not the wash please.'
To go downstairs to find the telephone.
'*Ring!* Pick me up, pick me up.'
I take a bowl from the cupboard
And place it on the side.
The cupboard door won't open.
Not today thank you.
The cereal is poured and my bowl's appetite is greedy for more.
I look out of the window.
Keep hunting, the sign says.

Sam Cowling (10)
Wellington Junior School, Wellington

Go To School

I got out of bed moaning and groaning
And attempted to get dressed.
My bed shouted and beckoned me back.
I resisted.
While staring at the table, I realised my bowl was empty
Starving to its base.
It screamed at me, 'Feed me, feed me!'
Slowly I picked up the cereal box.
It wriggled and refused to empty its contents.
My clothes seemed to hide from me in my wardrobe,
Sensing my reluctance.
I put on my shirt and did up my top button,
But it undid itself, 'Stop being stubborn!' I shouted.
Finally I did up the crying button.
I sprinted to the sink.
My toothbrush winked its bristly eyelash along my teeth.
In two minutes I was ready to go.
Run, jump in the car and I was out the house.
At last!

Alistair Matthews (11)
Wellington Junior School, Wellington

Friday Morning Feeling

I wake up to the angry shouts of my alarm clock.
I get up, but the mattress groans as if to say, 'Don't get up, don't get up.'
After I get down the stairs, the bowl screams
'Not me, not me, I've just been washed.'
I ignore his urgent pleas, and get on with my breakfast.
When that's done I clean my teeth and it purrs in satisfaction,
'Clean regularly, or I will report you to the dentist!'
I get dressed and look in the mirror,
It grins and reminds me of the scruffier times.
I grab my bag grumpily and in return,
It swings around and hits me on the back.
Moving out, I close the door quietly.
From above, the sun shines brightly down.
Now I am ready for the day and I hope it's ready for me.

Thomas Jeanes (11)
Wellington Junior School, Wellington

Getting Up!

I wake up as my dad shouts at me.
As my legs get attached to the floor, my bed seems to say, 'You're tired,
Remember, stay with me, I am warm and cosy.'
My legs crawl back into bed as my eyes are beginning to close.
Next thing my alarm clock starts screaming,
Shouting and screeching at me.
I hit it hard then it abruptly stops.
Nature calls - I head to the bathroom.
As I get there, my toothbrush maliciously scrapes my teeth,
Buzzing in delight.
I put up with it.
I walk down to the breakfast room and sit down.
Looking in the cupboard, all the cereal boxes eagerly push to the front,
Against each other.
They all seem to say, 'Pick me!'
I scowl at all my bags as I pick them up.
I climb into the car, the engine rumbles as my dad starts it up.
School awaits . . .

Imogen Hughes (11)
Wellington Junior School, Wellington

In The Morning

'C'mon mate, you've been in there for hours!'
My alarm clock seems to shout.
'I'm up, I'm up,' and I bash him on the head.
The carpet moans and the door creaks as I stumble out of bed.
I need a cup of tea . . . *now!*
The kettle gurgles and the teapot screams, 'Yeow! That's hot!'
My bowl struggles but is consumed by the milk.
Soon, the bowl is empty and my stomach stops complaining.
I wander upstairs to find my clothes snoring in the wardrobe.
With them finally on, into the bathroom.
'We'll wake you up,' the tooth cleaning utensils simper.
After I've brushed my teeth, I'm out of the front door, which is shivering from
the brisk night.
I step into the car and am ready to face another day of school.

Tom Brierley (11)
Wellington Junior School, Wellington

Alarming, Awakening

Time to get up dear,
She rings in my ear.

She whispers, you need to get up,
Before I get fed up.

She shouts and screams,
This is not your dreams.

Get up, get up you fool,
You need to go to school.

School today, 'No, no,'
I say, it's Sunday, not Monday.

Her head went down in shame,
If I get grumpy you'll get the blame!

Silence descended finally,
Into a peaceful, calming, melody.

Imogen Billington (11)
Wellington Junior School, Wellington

Monday Morning

My alarm clock yells into my ear.
I try to block his sound out but he mercilessly bombards me.
My bed moans and groans as I am forced out of it by my mum.
Upon entering the bathroom, my toothbrush robotically cleans my mouth,
Ignoring my drowsiness.
As I stumble downstairs, my bread leaps out of the toaster - it's hot in there!
My bacon screams on the grill - 'Burn baby, burn!'
I eat it all as my lunchbox stares hungrily at it.
I feed him my lunch and he devours it.
Nothing left after he gets it . . .
My wardrobe spits out my clothes as the mirror checks my hair.
The car growls and roars as it waits impatiently for passengers.
My bags hold on to my things like an octopus' sucker.
As the radiator relinquishes my sports kit, I cram it into my bag.
I'm ready at last!

Edward Peachey (10)
Wellington Junior School, Wellington

Brand New Day

My alarm clock begins to wail, but I ignore it,
Desperate to have another minute in bed.
It moans and groans until I wake up, but when I do,
My bed begs me to stay.
When I finally get up, I stare at myself in the mirror,
My reflection stares back at me with tired eyes from lack of sleep.
It seems to cackle, mocking and making fun of me.
I attempt to grab my clothes but they seem to wriggle away from me,
But at last they give in.
I am nearly dressed but now my tie slithers away from me
Like a coiled snake.
I creep down the creaking stairs to breakfast.
As I open the fridge it murmurs and hums like a purring cat.
I put the kettle on to boil and place the bread in the toaster.
The kettle began to squeal and whistle and, as if to accompany it,
Toast springs up and out, onto my plate.
I eat my toast and drink my tea quickly,
My stomach protests at this sudden rush of activity.
I grab my bags then rush off to school.
What a start to the day!

Abigail Reader (11)
Wellington Junior School, Wellington

Just An Ordinary Day

I wake up from the screaming of my alarm clock.
My hand drifts slowly and hits the button to stop its wailing
I slowly get out of my bed to get my clothes from the cupboard.
The floorboard groans under my weight as I stand on my tiptoes to open
the squeaking cupboard.
All the clothes tangle themselves, purposely annoying me.
The toilet groans at the smell of itself but nature calls.
I clean my teeth with my shivering, shaking and very loud toothbrush,
Before I head off downstairs to the kitchen.
On the wall there's lots of photos of me, clamouring for attention.
The cereal hides at the back of the cupboard, trying to get out of my reach.
Suddenly I look at the clock and realise I am late for school.
I run upstairs, get my bags and head off to school.

Samuel Edwards (11)
Wellington Junior School, Wellington

Mayhem!

'Wake up!' my alarm clock screamed,
'You will be late for school.'
My duvet stretched and yawned as I fell onto the floor!
The floorboards creaked and groaned as I tiptoed across the cold tiles.
The shower beckoned me in,
But in my peripheral vision the toilet winked.
'Don't I come before a shower?' it enquired.
Finished, I ran down the old crippled stairs,
Breakfast was calling my name,
I went to get the milk from the purring, contented fridge,
Pouring a sea of milk into my bowl,
I had successfully drowned my spoon,
I quickly ran back up the stairs,
And put on my tangled uniform,
Grabbed my bag,
What a morning of mayhem,
But finally, I left my house for school!

Alisa Gerasimidis (11)
Wellington Junior School, Wellington

Wake Up, Wake Up

'Ding-aling-ding-dong, cuckoo, wake up!'
It shouted, 'That's right you.'
My toothbrush beckoned me over,
'Time to wash your teeth,' it muttered,
'That's what you should do.'
It jumped up and down in the jar,
I blundered to the bedroom, my jumper shivered in the corner
That's where I got dressed.
I stuttered down the stairway like a clumsy baboon.
Sat down at the table
Pop went the toaster and out came the toast jumping and swaying in the air onto my plate.
Breakfast past,
Time was ticking
Half-seven already, time to go.
The car coughed and spluttered, gradually coming to life.
Here's to another fun day at school.

Patrick Buckley (10)
Wellington Junior School, Wellington

147

My Morning

I wake up one early morning.
To the sound of my alarm clock screaming and screeching.
So I whack him off my bedside table to shut him up for good.
I go to the lavatory, it tries to run for his life.
I quickly catch up with him and he groans like an old grandma because of the smell I have made.
Next I go into the shower, she doesn't even try to look at my bare body.
I come to my old pal, the toothbrush.
He is grinning at me as always and cleans my teeth perfectly.
I soon get changed and go downstairs, they groan in pain under my weight.
I sit in front of the TV, he gleams at me and says, 'Turn me on,' with his best grin.
Then I hear a rumbling noise outside.
What?
It is the dustbin - he is asking for garbage but I tell him straight. 'I don't have any,' I growl.
I put the kettle on for a few minutes until I hear a massive scream.
I have put her on for too long - oops!
Now she isn't much, but a black, burnt kettle - she doesn't look very impressed.
The clock suddenly bursts into a loud shout.
I am late for school!

Sebastian Woodhouse (10)
Wellington Junior School, Wellington

Morning Madness

Another morning, another argument.
'Get up, get up, you lazy person,' my alarm clock shrieks,
While my duvet is shouting, 'No stay in bed with me, I'm nice and warm.'
I eventually fall out of bed.
Dawdling towards my clothes,
I slowly put them on as they drag me to the floor.
I gaze into my no-nonsense mirror and it tells me the truth.
I look atrocious!
My hairbrush is soon trying to help me
By back-brushing my hair, scraping my scalp.
My toothpaste attacks my mouth with its extremely minty taste.
I steady myself whilst I stumble down the stairs.
They push and trip me up.
Open the old, crooked door that's pulling the other way.
My mum shouts loudly, 'Get here quickly, you slow coach.'
I hop to the car as my shoe refuses to go onto my foot.
I leap into the car and bang my toe on the door;
The car roars with impatience.
I am on my way to school.
Finally.

Lydia May (10)
Wellington Junior School, Wellington

Irritating Objects

I wake up and I feel like going back to bed.
My alarm clock yelps loudly into my ears.
It always seems to nag at me!
So I am forced to go down the moody stairs
That whisper softly from every direction.
I reach the bottom of the stairs - the whispering stops abruptly.
I open the breakfast cupboard.
'Pick me! Pick me!' the cereals all shout.
Whenever I pick one cereal, all the rest get louder!
I sprint up the stairs and get washed, as the sink kindly gurgles at me.
As I pull the plug, the gurgling gets louder and louder.
'Don't send me into the sewer!' it begs.
When I finally get changed, I run down the whispering stairs, as my tie
waves at me.
The velcro on my shoes screams in protest
As I rip the straps off and make them tighter.
I finally get into the car - it coughs as my mum starts the ignition.
Pretty much everything I possess is extremely irritating!

Ciaran Cheetham (11)
Wellington Junior School, Wellington

Morning Mayhem

My alarm clock rattles my bedside table to get me up.
I know that if I don't get up, he will get very fierce with me.
I pick up my abusive toothbrush.
My toothbrush cleans short and sharp.
It loses interest when I take too long so I place it back in its pot.
My toast jumps out of the toaster when it's good and ready.
My kettle whistles to me - fancy a cuppa?
I turn it off and drink a lovely cup of tea.
I open my cupboard and then I see all of my cereal
Rushing to get to the front.
'Pick me, pick me,' they all yelp.
My lunchbox is packed - it's tempting me in,
But I will wait patiently for lunchtime.
I climb into my trembling car - my dad turns on the engine.
Time to head for school.

Isabel Colman (11)
Wellington Junior School, Wellington

My Morning Trip To School

My alarm clock shrieks, my mattress groans,
'Get up, get up, it's time to go!'
The floorboards creak, the staircase moans,
'Hurry up, come on, you need to go!'
The cupboard swings open, the toaster pops up,
'Come on, get going, it's time to go!'
My tie pulls tight, he wriggles and squirms,
'Hurry up, come on, it's time to go!'
My shoes lead reluctantly to the door and,
I am up, I am ready, and I am set to go!

The door swings open, he shuts - goodbye,
I need to hurry - time is passing by!
My hat and coat tremble as I step outside,
I need to hurry, time is passing by!
My socks object as they get soaked with dew,
I have got minutes left as I speed into school!
My bag moans as she holds my books,
walking into class with nothing overlooked!

Fay Price (10)
Wellington Junior School, Wellington

Ice Cream World

In my ice cream world I can smell tasty ice cream flavours
Like vanilla, chocolate chip, coffee and strawberry and chocolate, yummy!

In my ice cream world I can hear ice cream melting
And chocolate waterfalls fall falling gracefully, falling calmly.

In my ice cream world I can see a chocolate ice cream cone
As a tree with chocolate flakes as branches
And candyfloss as leaves.

In my ice cream world touched a freezing cold ice cream
And it was as cold as a snowball
And I touched a colourful Smartie bridge.

In my ice cream world I tasted an ice cream
And it was so yummy
It was cold as an ice block.

Charlotte Simmons (9)
Windwhistle Primary School, Weston-super-Mare

War

In my war world it is as grey as a forty's photo
Screwed up in the corner of a dusty drawer.

In my war world I can taste horrible thick mud
As horrible as can be
As I crawl through the trenches.

In my war world I can feel danger creeping
Through my veins silently.

In my war world I can smell sweet smooth chocolate
In my peaceful dreams of happier times.

Bailey Bettle (9)
Windwhistle Primary School, Weston-super-Mare

The Dreadful Tower

In the dreadful tower I could smell rotten fruit which is mouldy and slimy
In an old, brown basket by the black, spider-webbed door.

In the dreadful tower, I could hear the guard dog sniffing the rotten fruit,
Which smells like an old man who hasn't had a bath for 53 years.

In the dreadful tower I could see the guard dogs jumping up fiercely
At the rusty old keys, which were as rusty as shiny metal
Rusting in the sun all day.

In the dreadful tower I could feel heavy, black chains on my wrist,
Which left a sore red mark on them.

In the dreadful tower I could taste fear in the air
Creeping all around me.

Clair Eyles (9)
Windwhistle Primary School, Weston-super-Mare

Shiny World

In my shiny world I can see a beautiful gold cloth doll
As a gold bar and she runs into my arms
And she runs slowly to the park.

In my shiny world I can hear wind howling as loud as a lion
And it is very strong and fierce.

In my shiny world I can smell a sweet apple pie as warm as the sun
The smell floats under my nose like a little lamb in summer,
It is a delightful smell.

In my shiny world I can feel a feathery bird as soft as a jumper,
It is as warm as a bath.

In my shiny world I can taste a sweet lollipop
As sweet as a piece of candyfloss, and it is tickling my tastebuds.

Ellen Thomas (9)
Windwhistle Primary School, Weston-super-Mare

Transformer World

In my Transformer world the cars are as cold
As being locked in the freezer for two nights.

In my Transformer world there are cars as tall as a skyscraper,
Even a little bit more.

In my Transformer world the cars are as dirty
As just getting pushed into a muddy puddle.

In my Transformer world, the Transformers stomp and make an awful lot of dust
And it goes in my mouth and it tastes disgusting.

In my Transformer world I can hear the Transformers from about three miles away
Because they are so noisy.

In my Transformer world I can smell burning rubber
From when they wheelspin for when they go to fight evil.

Jordan Toogood (9)
Windwhistle Primary School, Weston-super-Mare

The Magic Secret

In my secret world I can see magic drifting in the air.
I can see banana and strawberry gumdrops
Falling from the dark sky.

In my secret world, I can taste milky, soft chocolate flavour
Melting in my mouth.

In my secret world I can feel Dilisto's gumdrops falling in the chocolate pool
And the pop pool too.
I can feel a horse's tail like the river.

In my secret world I can hear chocolate fall
And some butterflies fluttering.

In my secret world I can hear the clouds moving.

Kasey Cornish (8)
Windwhistle Primary School, Weston-super-Mare

My Manchester United World

In my Manchester United world I can smell freshly planted grass
Wafting past my nose gently.

In my Manchester United world I can hear bright lights
Buzzing in the gloomy sky.

In my Manchester United world I can see bright red seats
Which are as clean as rain.

In my Manchester United world I can feel the dark, damp concrete
Which stands as hard as rock in the gloomy night.

In my Manchester United world I can taste the bitter wheezy air
In the mystical sky.

Harrison Deady (8)
Windwhistle Primary School, Weston-super-Mare

Factory World

In my factory world I can smell thick, black oil
Burning strong, steaming and stinking.

In my factory world I can hear spots of oil
Dripping gracefully in a pitter-patter pattern.

In my factory world I can feel shiny walls
As shiny as glistening metal, shining in the beautiful summer sun.

In my factory world I can taste disgusting, filthy dust
From the huge machines and floating like a butterfly.

In my factory world I can see tall, huge and metal towers
And enormous thundering machines working for their lives.

Dray Bird (8)
Windwhistle Primary School, Weston-super-Mare

My Jungle World

In my jungle world I can
Smell beautiful, colourful flowers growing
By a lovely, twinkling lake.

In my jungle world I can
Hear a black jaguar roaring and running,
As fast as a flash.

In my jungle world I can see
A person swinging happily through the treetops.

In my jungle world I can
Touch the tasty bananas.

In my jungle world I can
Taste the sweet juicy strawberries in the tall high trees
The trees are as green as the grass.

Joseph Rutter (8)
Windwhistle Primary School, Weston-super-Mare

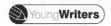

My Rabbit World

In my rabbit world I can
Smell the disgusting pong of hundreds of small, round, brown rabbit droppings.

In my rabbit world I can
Hear the sound of long, sharp, shiny claws furiously scratching
Like a cat with a woollen ball.

In my rabbit world I can
Touch the soft, silky, rainbow-coloured fur.

In my rabbit world I can see
Wood shavings as rough as coarse sandpaper.

In my rabbit world I can
Taste the orange, tingly sensation of a crunchy carrot.

Alicia Buck (8)
Windwhistle Primary School, Weston-super-Mare

Winter Wonderland

In my winter wonderland
I can feel my skates gliding and sliding gracefully
Like a beautiful golden swan.

In my winter wonderland
I can taste delicious fudge ice cream
Covered all over with crunchy chocolate chips.

Emily Bell (8)
Windwhistle Primary School, Weston-super-Mare

My Time Frozen World

In my time frozen world I can smell the sweet smell of roses
Wafting gently in the air.

In my time frozen world I can hear the sound of deep blue water
Crashing fiercely like a monster.

In my time frozen world I can see swirling swamps
Full of slithering slippery snakes.

In my time frozen world I can taste electric-charged particles
Tickling my tongue excitedly.

In my time frozen world I can touch the icy frozen clocks
As cold as a deep frozen river.

Keanu Toomer (8)
Windwhistle Primary School, Weston-super-Mare

In My Magical World

In my magical world
I can smell the stench of rotten corpses covered in blood,
Lying in a pile on the battlefield.

In my marvellous magical world
I can see spears flying through the air like lightning.

In my magical world
I can hear an eerie silence creeping over the battlefield.

In my magical world
I touched an evil, green goblin that twitched horribly
And burst into flames and transformed into a skeleton.

In my magical world
I can taste endless tides of fear rippling over my tongue.

Daniel Powell (8)
Windwhistle Primary School, Weston-super-Mare

Featured Author:

Maddie Stewart

Maddie is a children's writer, poet and author who currently lives in Coney Island, Northern Ireland.

Maddie has 5 published children's books, 'Cinders', 'Hal's Sleepover', 'Bertie Rooster', 'Peg' and 'Clever Daddy'. Maddie uses her own unpublished work to provide entertaining, interactive poems and rhyming stories for use in her workshops with children when she visits schools, libraries, arts centres and book festivals.

Favourites are 'Silly Billy, Auntie Millie' and 'I'm a Cool, Cool Kid'. Maddie works throughout Ireland from her home in County Down. She is also happy to work from a variety of bases in England. She has friends and family, with whom she regularly stays, in Leicester, Bedford, London and Ashford (Kent). Maddie's workshops are aimed at 5-11-year-olds. Check out Maddie's website for all her latest news and free poetry resources **www.maddiestewart.com**.

Read on to pick up some fab writing tips!

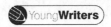

Nonsense Workshop

**If you find silliness fun,
you will love nonsense poems.
Nonsense poems might describe silly things,
or people, or situations,
or, any combination of the three.**

For example:

When I got out of bed today,
both my arms had run away.
I sent my feet to fetch them back.
When they came back, toe in hand
I realised what they had planned.
They'd made the breakfast I love most,
buttered spider's eggs on toast.

**One way to find out if you enjoy nonsense poems
is to start with familiar nursery rhymes.
Ask your teacher to read them out,
putting in the names of some children in your class.**

Like this: Troy and Jill went up the hill
to fetch a pail of water.
Troy fell down
and broke his crown
and Jill came tumbling after.

If anyone is upset at the idea of using their name, then don't use it.

Did you find this fun?

Now try changing a nursery rhyme.
Keep the rhythm and the rhyme style, but invent a silly situation.

Like this: Hickory Dickory Dare
a pig flew up in the air.
The clouds above
gave him a shove
Hickory Dickory Dare.

Or this: Little Miss Mabel
sat at her table
eating a strawberry pie
but a big, hairy beast
stole her strawberry feast
and made poor little Mabel cry.

How does your rhyme sound if you put your own name in it?

Another idea for nonsense poems is to pretend letters are people
and have them do silly things.

For example:

Mrs A	Mrs B	Mrs C
Lost her way	Dropped a pea	Ate a tree

To make your own 'Silly People Poem', think of a word to use.
To show you an example, I will choose the word 'silly'.
Write your word vertically down the left hand side of your page.
Then write down some words which rhyme
with the sound of each letter.

S mess, dress, Bess, chess, cress
I eye, bye, sky, guy, pie, sky
L sell, bell, shell, tell, swell, well
L " " " " " (" means the same as written above)
Y (the same words as those rhyming with I)

Use your rhyming word lists to help you make up your poem.

Mrs S made a mess
Mrs I ate a pie
Mrs L rang a bell
Mrs L broke a shell
Mrs Y said 'Bye-bye.'

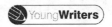

**You might even make a 'Silly Alphabet' by using
all the letters of the alphabet.**

**It is hard to find rhyming words for all the letters.
H, X and W are letters which are hard to match with rhyming words.
I'll give you some I've thought of:**

H - cage, stage, wage (close but not perfect)
X - flex, specs, complex, Middlesex
W - trouble you, chicken coop, bubble zoo

**However, with nonsense poems, you can use nonsense words.
You can make up your own words.**

**To start making up nonsense words you could
try mixing dictionary words together.
Let's make up some nonsense animals.**

Make two lists of animals. (You can include birds and fish as well.)

Your lists can be as long as you like. These are lists I made:

elephant	kangaroo
tiger	penguin
lizard	octopus
monkey	chicken

**Now use the start of an animal on one list and substitute
it for the start of an animal from your other list.**

I might use the start of oct/opus ... oct and substitute it for the end of l/izard
to give me a new nonsense animal ... an octizard.
I might swap the start of monk/ey ... monk with the end of kang/aroo
To give me another new nonsense animal ... a monkaroo.

What might a monkaroo look like? What might it eat?

**You could try mixing some food words in the same way,
to make up nonsense foods.**

cabbage	potatoes
lettuce	parsley
bacon	crisps

**Cribbage, bacley, and lettatoes are some nonsense foods
made up from my lists.**

Let's see if I can make a nonsense poem about my monkaroo.

My monkaroo loves bacley.
He'll eat lettatoes too
But his favourite food is cribbage
Especially if it's blue.

Would you like to try and make up your own nonsense poem?

**Nonsense words don't have to be a combination of dictionary words.
They can be completely 'made up'.
You can use nonsense words to write nonsense sonnets,
or list poems or any type of poem you like.**

Here is a poem full of nonsense words:

I melly micked a turdle
and flecked a pendril's tum.
I plotineyed a shugat
and dracked a pipin's plum.

**Ask your teacher to read it putting in some children's names instead
of the first I, and he or she instead of the second I.**

Did that sound funny?

You might think that nonsense poems are just silly and not for the serious poet.
However poets tend to love language. Making up your own words is a natural
part of enjoying words and sounds and how they fit together. Many poets love the
freedom nonsense poems give them. Lots and lots of very famous poets have written
nonsense poems. I'll name some: **Edward Lear**, **Roger McGough**, **Lewis Carroll**,
Jack Prelutsky and **Nick Toczek**. Can you or your teacher think of any more?
For help with a class nonsense poem or to find more nonsense nursery rhymes look
on my website, **www.maddiestewart.com**. Have fun! Maddie Stewart.

POETRY TECHNIQUES

HERE IS a SELECTION OF POETRY TECHNIQUES WITH EXAMPLES

Metaphors & Similes

A *metaphor* is when you describe your subject *as* something else, for example:
'Winter is a cruel master leaving the servants in a bleak wilderness'
whereas a *simile* describes your subject *like* something else i.e.
'His blue eyes are like ice-cold puddles' or 'The flames flickered like eyelashes'.

Personification

This is to simply give a personality to something that is not human, for example
'Fear spreads her uneasiness around' or 'Summer casts down her warm sunrays'.

Imagery

To use words to create mental pictures of what you are trying to convey,
your poem should awaken the senses and make the reader
feel like they are in that poetic scene …
'The sky was streaked with pink and red as shadows
cast across the once-golden sand'.
'The sea gently lapped the shore as the palm trees rustled softly
in the evening breeze'.

Assonance & Alliteration

Alliteration uses a repeated constant sound and this effect can be quite striking:
'Smash, slippery snake slithered sideways'.
Assonance repeats a significant vowel or vowel sound to create an impact:
'The pool looked cool'.

Poetry Techniques

Repetition

By repeating a significant word the echo effect can be a very powerful way of enhancing an emotion or point your poem is putting across.
'The blows rained down, down,
Never ceasing,
Never caring
About the pain,
The pain'.

Onomatopoeia

This simply means you use words that sound like the noise you are describing, for example 'The rain *pattered* on the window' or 'The tin can *clattered* up the alley'.

Rhythm & Metre

The *rhythm* of a poem means 'the beat', the sense of movement you create. The placing of punctuation and the use of syllables affect the *rhythm* of the poem. If your intention is to have your poem read slowly, use double, triple or larger syllables and punctuate more often, where as if you want to have a fast-paced read use single syllables, less punctuation and shorter sentences.
If you have a regular rhythm throughout your poem this is known as *metre*.

Enjambment

This means you don't use punctuation at the end of your line, you simply let the line flow on to the next one. It is commonly used and is a good word to drop into your homework!

Tone & Lyric

The poet's intention is expressed through their *tone*. You may feel happiness, anger, confusion, loathing or admiration for your poetic subject. Are you criticising or praising? How you feel about your topic will affect your choice of words and therefore your *tone*. For example 'I *loved* her', 'I *cared* for her', 'I *liked* her'.
If you write the poem from a personal view or experience this is referred to as a *lyrical* poem. A good example of a lyrical poem is Seamus Heaney's 'Mid-term Break' or any sonnet!

All About Shakespeare

Try this fun quiz with your family, friends or even in class!

1. Where was Shakespeare born?

....

2. Mercutio is a character in which Shakepeare play?

....

3. Which monarch was said to be 'quite a fan' of his work?

....

4. How old was he when he married?

....

5. What is the name of the last and 'only original' play he wrote?

....

6. What are the names of King Lear's three daughters?

....

7. Who is Anne Hathaway?

....

8. Which city is the play 'Othello' set in?

....

9. Can you name 2 of Shakespeare's 17 comedies?

....

10. 'This day is call'd the feast of Crispian: He that outlives this day, and comes safe home, Will stand a tip-toe when this day is nam'd, and rouse him at the name of Crispian' is a quote from which play?

....

11. Leonardo DiCaprio played Romeo in the modern day film version of Romeo and Juliet. Who played Juliet in the movie?

....

12. Three witches famously appear in which play?

....

13. Which famous Shakespearean character is Eric in the image to the left?

....

14. What was Shakespeare's favourite poetic form?

....

Answers are printed on the last page of the book, good luck!

If you would rather try the quiz online, you can do so at www.youngwriters.co.uk.

Poetry Activity

Word Soup

**To help you write a poem, or even a story,
on any theme, you should create word soup!**

If you have a theme or subject for your poem, base your word soup on it.
If not, don't worry, the word soup will help you find a theme.

To start your word soup you need ingredients:

- Nouns (names of people, places, objects, feelings, i.e. Mum, Paris, house, anger)
- Colours
- Verbs ('doing words', i.e. kicking, laughing, running, falling, smiling)
- Adjectives (words that describe nouns, i.e. tall, hairy, hollow, smelly, angelic)

We suggest at least 5 of each from the above list, this will make sure your word soup
has plenty of choice. Now, if you have already been given a theme or title for your
poem, base your ingredients on this. If you have no idea what to write about,
write down whatever you like, or ask a teacher or family member to give you
a theme to write about.

Poetry Activity

Making Word Soup

Next, you'll need a sheet of paper.
Cut it into at least 20 pieces. Make sure the pieces are big enough to write your ingredients on, one ingredient on each piece of paper.
Write your ingredients on the pieces of paper.
Shuffle the pieces of paper and put them all in a box or bowl
- something you can pick the paper out of without looking at the words.
Pick out 5 words to start and use them to write your poem!

Example:

Our theme is winter. Our ingredients are:
- Nouns: snowflake, Santa, hat, Christmas, snowman.
- Colours: blue, white, green, orange, red.
- Verbs: ice-skating, playing, laughing, smiling, wrapping.
- Adjectives: cold, tall, fast, crunchy, sparkly.

**Our word soup gave us these 5 words:
snowman, red, cold, hat, fast and our poem goes like this:**

It's a *cold* winter's day,
My nose and cheeks are *red*
As I'm outside, building my *snowman*,
I add a *hat* and a carrot nose to finish,
I hope he doesn't melt too *fast*!

**Tip: add more ingredients to your word soup
and see how many different poems you can write!**

**Tip: if you're finding it hard to write a poem with
the words you've picked, swap a word with another one!**

**Tip: try adding poem styles and techniques,
such as assonance or haiku to your soup for an added challenge!**

SCRIBBLER!

YOUNG WRITERS INFORMATION

We hope you have enjoyed reading this
book - and that you will continue to enjoy it
in the coming years.

If you like reading and writing poetry drop
us a line, or give us a call, and we'll send
you a free information pack.

Alternatively, if you would like to order further
copies of this book or any of our other titles,
then please give us a call or log onto our
website at www.youngwriters.co.uk.

Young Writers Information
Remus House
Coltsfoot Drive
Peterborough
PE2 9BF
Tel: (01733) 890066
Fax: (01733) 313524

Email: info@youngwriters.co.uk